An important book addressing an important problem. It helped me understand myself better.

—Rabbi Harold Kushner, author of *When Bad Things Happen to Good People*

The notion of retirement as a time of withdrawal is largely disappearing. In its place is a new, much more vital vision of how most people want to live as they grow older. *Don't Retire, REWIRE!*™ offers anyone contemplating retirement practical steps for realizing this new vision of retirement as a time to begin a new chapter, start new activities, and set new goals.

—William D. Novelli, executive director and CEO of AARP

None of us spends enough time thinking and planning for retirement. *Don't Retire, REWIRE!*™ is an awakening for anyone who has ever wondered "Who will I be?" when traditional work or career ends. This book will inspire and offer insight into the possibilities that are out there.

—Helen R. Hamlin, MSSW, ACSW, main representative to the United Nations, International Federation on Aging, chair, NGO Committee on Aging, United Nations, New York

It is a familiar truism to say that "the human being was never intended to live this long" (as we do in the twenty-first century). A friend of mine puts it in a better way. "Biology," she likes to say, "will only take you to age 50. After that, you have to give yourself a reason for living." Jeri and Rick have written a manual to help those who are willing to work hard at finding a reason for living beyond 50. I think the manual is helpful. I commend it to you.

—Richard N. Bolles, author of *What Color Is Your Parachute?* (2002)

Don't Retire, REWIRE!™ is for leaders who want to be a success even when not working full-time. For those who want to use their portfolio of talents to ensure success lasts a lifetime, *Don't Retire, REWIRE!*™ is a road map to future fulfillment.

—Wally O'Brien, former director general, International Advertising Association

Many of us are so engaged in our day-to-day lives that we don't have an opportunity to recognize and savor those things that bring us true satisfaction. *Don't Retire, REWIRE!*™ serves as a catalyst to focusing on the activities that bring us meaning. Whether rethinking a current career or planning the next chapter, you will be stimulated to take steps to concentrate your activities on those things that bring rewards.

—Barbara Berger Opotowsky, *Esquire*

My experience making portraits for the Elder Grace project has taught me that the people who maintain a sense of purpose in their lives glow with a passion for living. Their souls radiate an interior completeness that translates into photographs of dignified joy. Look beyond traditional retirement and redefine your "elder" career. *Don't Retire, REWIRE!*™ gives you the ideas and the steps for finding your purpose and your glow.

—Chester Higgins Jr., photographer/author, *Elder Grace: The Nobility of Aging* (Bulfinch, 2000) and staff photographer for *The New York Times*

Before 9/11, there was much talk of people seeking meaning in their lives. After that date, the desire for meaning evolved to include making a difference and having increased personal fulfillment. These desires show that something much more basic is gnawing at a significant portion of the population—relevance. *Don't Retire, REWIRE!*™ is for those foresighted people who want to discover what really motivates and fulfills them so they can craft the most relevant "next act" for themselves.

—Edie Weiner, futurist, trends analysis, president, Weiner, Edrich Brown

Doctors are so overfocused and overworked that they never consider intelligent retirement options. *Don't Retire, REWIRE!*™ is their much-needed missing link for the creation of a successful exit strategy and fulfillment in their "golden years."

—Dr. Al Kurpis

Don't Retire, REWIRE!™

Second Edition

Don't Retire, REWIRE!™

5 Steps to Fulfilling Work That Fuels Your Passion, Suits Your Personality, and Fills Your Pocket

Second Edition

Jeri Sedlar and Rick Miners

ALPHA

A member of Penguin Group (USA) Inc.

ALPHA BOOKS

Published by the Penguin Group

Penguin Group (USA) Inc., 375 Hudson Street, New York, New York 10014, USA

Penguin Group (Canada), 90 Eglinton Avenue East, Suite 700, Toronto, Ontario M4P 2Y3, Canada (a division of Pearson Penguin Canada Inc.)

Penguin Books Ltd., 80 Strand, London WC2R 0RL, England

Penguin Ireland, 25 St. Stephen's Green, Dublin 2, Ireland (a division of Penguin Books Ltd.)

Penguin Group (Australia), 250 Camberwell Road, Camberwell, Victoria 3124, Australia (a division of Pearson Australia Group Pty. Ltd.)

Penguin Books India Pvt. Ltd., 11 Community Centre, Panchsheel Park, New Delhi—110 017, India

Penguin Group (NZ), 67 Apollo Drive, Rosedale, North Shore, Auckland 1311, New Zealand (a division of Pearson New Zealand Ltd.)

Penguin Books (South Africa) (Pty.) Ltd., 24 Sturdee Avenue, Rosebank, Johannesburg 2196, South Africa

Penguin Books Ltd., Registered Offices: 80 Strand, London WC2R 0RL, England

International Standard Book Number: 978-1-59257-689-0
Library of Congress Catalog Card Number: 2007928984

09   08   8   7   6   5   4   3   2

Interpretation of the printing code: The rightmost number of the first series of numbers is the year of the book's printing; the rightmost number of the second series of numbers is the number of the book's printing. For example, a printing code of 07-1 shows that the first printing occurred in 2007.

Printed in the United States of America

Note: This publication contains the opinions and ideas of its authors. It is intended to provide helpful and informative material on the subject matter covered. It is sold with the understanding that the authors and publisher are not engaged in rendering professional services in the book. If the reader requires personal assistance or advice, a competent professional should be consulted.

The authors and publisher specifically disclaim any responsibility for any liability, loss, or risk, personal or otherwise, which is incurred as a consequence, directly or indirectly, of the use and application of any of the contents of this book.

Trademarks: All terms mentioned in this book that are known to be or are suspected of being trademarks or service marks have been appropriately capitalized. Alpha Books and Penguin Group (USA) Inc. cannot attest to the accuracy of this information. Use of a term in this book should not be regarded as affecting the validity of any trademark or service mark.

Rewire[TM]*; Don't Retire, REWIRE*[TM]*;* and *Rewirement*® are the trademarks of Jeri Sedlar.

Most Alpha books are available at special quantity discounts for bulk purchases for sales promotions, premiums, fund-raising, or educational use. Special books, or book excerpts, can also be created to fit specific needs.

For details, write: Special Markets, Alpha Books, 375 Hudson Street, New York, NY 10014.

Contents

Foreword

Imagine someone who worked for 40 years as a productive engineer, or marketing executive, or highly involved community leader, housewife, and mother, who now lives alone, isolated, in "retirement." What happens to the biology of that person's brain when there is a lack of stimulation and a cessation of learning and social interaction?

Perhaps more important, what happens to her quality of life? What is the meaning of a "purposeless" old age? And what are the societal implications of an increasing number of older individuals leading unproductive lives?

As a geriatrician caring for older persons, the greatest challenge I face in my private practice is not whether I can manage a patient's hypertension or diabetes. Once I have answered all the questions about their medical illnesses, I usually bring the conversation around to asking them the really important questions: "What will you do with the rest of your life? Despite your illnesses, how will you achieve some quality of life, some daily contribution that gives you meaning and purpose?" Most of the time, there are few answers to these questions regarding what gerontologists call "productive aging."

I met Jeri Sedlar after a speech I delivered on "Achieving and Maintaining Cognitive Vitality in Late Life" at The Rockefeller University in New York City. She asked me if there are really things people can do to stay vital and productive with aging. When she told me about her idea for this book, I encouraged her.

Don't Retire, REWIRE!™ was written because millions of people over age 50 need to know what they can do to achieve a future they can look forward to, if they think ahead and act. Many people approach their later years worried about cognitive decline, increasing social isolation, and loss of meaningful and productive activities. In contrast, others look forward to the years past 65 as a vital, active time in their lives. Some postpone retirement. Others choose to travel, volunteer, or begin new careers and adapt the philosophy "to enjoy everyday life fully." Recent data indicates that mental exercise and activity are important in preventing cognitive decline. Like muscles, "use it or lose it" applies equally to the brain. (See more information at www.aging-institute.org.)

As experts in executive search and development, Jeri and Rick have applied their unique knowledge and perspective to the field of retirement. Just as they counseled those going through midlife stages of career development, they now counsel aging boomers and older persons who need to discover their personal motivations to use in planning the last third of life, which may last 30 years. The authors have recognized the importance of this knowledge for selecting one's activities and defining one's direction for this later period of life.

For the longevity revolution, productive aging is critical to individuals and to society. Older individuals need to feel productive, and society needs productive older persons. To achieve quality of life, meaning, and significance with aging, older persons need to continue to acquire new knowledge and experience and to remain active at home, at work, and in their communities. *Don't Retire, REWIRE!*™ is a road map, a personal manual, to help maturing people achieve productive aging.

Howard Fillit, M.D.
Executive Director, The Institute for the Study of Aging
www.aging-institute.org

Preface

When *Don't Retire, REWIRE!*™ was first published in 2002, the oldest boomer had not yet turned 60, and the idea of redefining retirement to include fulfilling work was only beginning to come on people's screens. Today it's a different story. The rewiring process we created has turned into a rewiring trend, and more and more people want to become part of the *rewire* generation.

Since the first edition was published, we have been traveling the country, delivering programs on how to *rewire* to the clients of financial institutions, business owners and partnerships, residents of active retirement communities, at hospitals, churches, senior centers, and within corporations. We have met thousands of people and heard about how they're rewiring, about their new possibilities, about the opportunities they've discovered, and even about their frustrations. It was questions and comments from attendees at our presentations, combined with readers' questions, conversations with retirees and pre-retirees, and our own tracking of emerging trends that led us to update *Don't Retire, REWIRE!*™ The new edition includes a revised Chapter 12 and a new Chapter 13. A summary of feedback we received from people we've met is included in a new Appendix A, "The Ten Nuggets of Knowledge to Enhance Your Rewiring."

People are getting our message that life planning in conjunction with financial planning is the ticket to a fulfilling future. Increased longevity—the additional 20 to 25 years that we could live *after the age of 65*—is the rationale for the rewiring trend. An estimated 3 million boomers will live to be 100 (compared to 55,000 who live to be 100 today!). Just as important as financial concerns are questions about how to be engaged in "meaningful" "work" (however one chooses to define "meaningful" and "work"). What is the role of the employer? Of the individual? How will people find a new community that is engaging and fulfilling? What are the new workplace realities? What are the particular concerns of married couples? And how does one discover new purpose in retirement?

We've observed that the idea of living so much longer evokes a broad range of emotions in people—from realistic to optimistic to downright pessimistic! For the people who have hobbies, passions, and dreams, the longevity bonus is a gift. But for those without, it's not a gift, but, as one man told us, "It's a curse!"

We come down firmly on the positive side and hope this new edition will continue to help you find and enjoy fulfillment in your rewired life.

Get ready to *rewire* your future. It can be all you want it to be.

Jeri and Rick

Introduction

One day we got a telephone call that surprised us. One of our corporate clients, a man named Bill, age 59, called and said, "You've always given me great career advice. How about some help when I *quit* working?" He explained, "I used to look forward to retirement … see it as a reward for all my years of hard work, but now that it's getting closer, I'm not so sure."

As executive search consultants, we had worked with Bill both as a job candidate and as a client for whom we found job candidates. He was a high-energy, creative problem-solver who loved a challenge. His current job as a senior manager in a Fortune 100 technology company was stable and included a nice pension. Even with the volatility of the stock market, Bill would be able to financially support a nice retirement. *What kind of help did he need?* we wondered.

When we sat down to talk with Bill, we began to understand. Bill revealed that he had seen his dad retire into a life of golf and the golf-club social scene. Bill liked golf, but he needed more. He had come to realize that a traditional retirement like his father's was not for him. He wanted to do something productive—but he didn't know what. He just knew he didn't want anything as demanding as the 24/7 existence he had been living for the past three years. He told us that he "dreamed about working on his own terms, on his own schedule." He asked us if there was anything like that out there. And if so, how could he find it?

We put our heads together and explored Bill's vision in greater detail. We used our 25 years of executive search and counseling experience and shared our own personal brand of "letting-the-kite-out thinking" to help him identify a range of work choices—from volunteer to entrepreneurial—he could begin to investigate while he was still working. By the time we were done, because we had brainstormed ideas that played right into his professional and personal "hot buttons," Bill was able to see opportunities he didn't realize would be there for him when he retired. We worked with several more clients, all of whom shared some of the same dreams and concerns as Bill. With each one, we shared the key secret for success: *know what you'll be leaving behind when you retire and then figure out how to replace that in the future.*

That was how the idea for this book was born.

Although we had helped many people successfully plot their retirement success, we wanted to discover how and what current retirees and pre-retirees were thinking so we could learn from their experiences. We conducted focus groups, surveys, and personal interviews with more than 200 pre-retirees (age 39 to 77) and more than 100 working and nonworking retirees (age 41 to 99) across the United States. The names of people used as examples in the following pages have been changed to protect their privacy.

Our research focused on the lifestyle side of retirement, not the financial side. We knew there were already many good financial books on the market, not to mention financial planners offering sound advice. Our primary focus is on the aspect of retirement most people either ignore or can't face: what will I *do?* The process we've laid out in this book works whether or not you have enough (or nearly enough) money for retirement (whatever that amount is for you).

In our research, we interviewed many people, both retirees and pre-retirees, who were dissatisfied with the concept of traditional retirement with its focus on leisure. We met others who were not only satisfied, but had created a new kind of retirement for themselves. We realized that these happy people had either intuitively known what their deepest needs were—and had fulfilled them with new activities— or had discovered how to satisfy them through trial and error. Either way, they had found ways to meet their needs after they retired. We studied these people closely and examined their instinctive "method."

Our research showed that most people hate the word *retirement,* so we decided to rename this highly satisfying alternative to traditional retirement, *rewirement,* and the alternative to retiring, *rewiring.* To *rewire* is to reroute personal energy you spent on full-time work into deeply satisfying, personally customized work activities (full-time, part-time, flex-time, phased, sabbatical, seasonal, paid, personal, and/or volunteer) that can transform your next act into the most fulfilling time of your life. The satisfied people who chose the alternative to traditional retirement are *rewirees.* Their stories, combined with our expertise, are the basis for this book.

The five steps of the *rewire* process—a formula we have used successfully with our clients—are as follows:

1. Seeing the opportunity: retiring is a going *from,* and rewiring is a going *to.*
2. Identifying your "drivers."
3. Linking the drivers to your activities.

4. Creating your rewired vision.

5. Developing your action plan.

This book is intended to be interactive, and as you progress through it, you'll see that principles developed in later chapters rely on themes developed in earlier chapters.

You'll be confronted with some personal and thought-provoking questions throughout the book, so we ask you to keep a journal in which to write your answers.

In Chapter 1, we introduce you to some people who retired the old way and "flunked" retirement. You'll also meet four pre-retirees—Tom, Paula, Bob, and Carol—who reject the traditional definition of retirement and are rewiring. We track them throughout the book, following their progress as they *rewire*, and watch them shape their transformed lives. You'll see how they all expanded the traditional definition of *work* and customized their options in a way that met their deepest needs, visions, and values. Like them, you can write your own next act. A world of exciting choices can be yours, if you're willing to begin your journey with the first step.

Acknowledgments

We'd like to thank the more than 300 people—clients, friends, and associates—who were so wonderful in sharing their thoughts, fears, questions, expectations, and self-revealing stories with us. They contributed greatly to the foundation of this book. To those who allowed us to follow their personal journeys, we will always be grateful.

A big thank you to Martha Jewett (www.marthajewett.com), our wonderful agent and editorial consultant, for believing in us and helping us develop the book concept. She deserves the highest praise for her persistence, sense of humor, and focus.

The warmest thanks ever to Laure Aubuchon, our Boswell. You got us through many challenges, and we'll never forget it.

Special thanks to Irene Cohen, Wally O'Brien, Dr. Muriel Vogel, and Bruce Ellig—rewirees who continue to inspire us! And to Dr. Tessa Warschaw, Karen Walden, Mike Guarini, Doreen Frasca, and Sally Paynter, who read various versions of this book and gave us valuable input. We also give a hearty thank you to Anita Lands, a great teacher, coach, and new friend.

Sincere thanks go to Dr. Howard Fillit, executive director of the Institute for the Study on Aging. Praise and thanks go to our dear and brilliant friend, Marc Myers.

Big thanks go to friends Debra Flanz, Pam Laudenslager, Andrea Nierenberg, Griff and Carole Foxley, and Melinda Wolfe, who were always there cheering us on, along with Amy Friedman, Gail Blanke, Brad and Sue Bremer, Jane Applegate, and Suzanne Dowling, who offered support just when it was needed.

Thanks to the whole team at Alpha, who have been terrific in making this book readable and relevant, and the journey painless: Mike Sanders, Marie Butler-Knight, and Christy Wagner.

And a big thank you to all the thoughtful friends, acquaintances, and colleagues who offered encouragement along the way. You know who you are, and we appreciate you.

Thank you to Jeri's mother, Helen, and Rick's mother, Alice, who continue to inspire and delight.

Step 1

Seeing the Opportunity:
Retiring Is a Going *From,* and
Rewiring Is a Going *To*

Chapter 1
Flunking Retirement

I hate the word retirement. *My dad retired; I won't retire.*
—*Nick, 50, CPA*

Traditional retirement isn't for everyone. Take, for example, Dan and Arlene, a couple we've known for years and bumped into recently. Dan had had a very successful career as an attorney in New York City, and Arlene had been an accountant. They had retired a year before and moved to the south of France, to a beautiful spot they had visited on four prior dream vacations. In France, they planned to live out their perfect vision of retirement: museum hopping to do some sketching and painting, visiting with friends, cooking with the freshest herbs and ingredients.

"What are you doing here?" I said. "We heard you retired to France."

"It was horrible," Arlene said.

"Not us," Dan agreed.

"We flunked retirement," they said together, laughing.

"What do you mean?" I asked.

Arlene thought for a moment, searching for the right words. Then her eyes widened. "We missed our lives!"

"We Flunked Retirement"

"We flunked retirement" made us stop and think. How could two smart people with all the means in the world have "flunked" retirement? Where had they gone wrong? We were puzzled about this and asked Dan and Arlene to talk with us further. When we met with them, they explained that their life had turned into an endless vacation—a lifestyle they had thought would be right for them, but wasn't. They admitted that during the 20 months they had spent in the south of France, they had learned a lot about themselves and what makes them tick.

Before retirement, Dan and Arlene had both been active in community and philanthropic activities. They had family nearby whom they saw frequently. They had regular routines. Dan played racquetball twice a week with an old friend. Arlene regularly took her grandchildren on special outings, like going to see *The Nutcracker* at Christmas.

Of course, they had realized before they retired that they would no longer be able to do these things in France, but it had never occurred to them that they would miss them so much. Dan and Arlene realized that they had given up too much of what they loved.

Finally, it dawned on Dan and Arlene that they hadn't needed to go to the south of France to find retirement satisfaction. It was in their own backyard. All they had to do to find it was know themselves better.

" Real Quotes

Lee Iacocca said that he flunked retirement. In a famous *Fortune* magazine article (June 24, 1996), the retired Chrysler executive warned, "You plan everything in life, and then the roof caves in on you because you haven't done enough thinking about who you are and what you should do with the rest of your life."

Traditional Retirement Is Outmoded

Traditional retirement, in the old sense of leisure only, isn't
for everyone. Because of the ways the world has changed, and
for reasons we talk more about later in this chapter, traditional
retirement isn't something you should accept without careful
thought.

Retirement has traditionally meant a going *from*. The traditional meaning of retirement is a single event—"withdrawal"
from the workforce into leisure, relaxation, a slide into the end
of life. *Webster's* dictionary defines retirement as "removal or
withdrawal from an office or active service; to seek privacy or
seclusion." The word *retire* comes from the French word *retirer,*
meaning "to withdraw," which comes from the French verb *tirer,*
meaning "drawing out or enduring," the same root "martyr"
comes from. Not exactly inspiring!

Even the words associated with retirement are inadequate. *Semi-
retirement* doesn't suffice (although we use the term because there's
no other alternative yet). The term *middle-aged workplace issues* totally
misses the point. *Second-career itch* sounds like change for the sake of
change. *Early retirement* is a euphemism for executives who are laid
off. *Un-retire* sounds too much like the un-cola! In fact, the subject
of this book—working in retirement—would have been considered
an oxymoron until just a few years ago. An article on retirement
in *American Demographics* magazine had this to say about the word:
"The dictionary often has trouble keeping up with society's changing definitions of traditional nomenclature, but perhaps the term
'retirement' needs to be retired altogether."[1]

Society has changed. Retirement was invented by Bismarck, first
chancellor of the German Empire, in the late nineteenth century,
when most people didn't live long enough to worry about what they
were going to do when they stopped working. Even when Social
Security was instituted in the United States in 1935, benefits began
at 65 but the average life expectancy was only 61!

❝❝ **Real Quotes**

Jimmy Carter calls his 1980 presidential defeat his "involuntary retirement." When he went home to Plains, Georgia, he was 56. "I realized that according to the life expectancy tables, I had 25 years to go. What was I going to do with 25 more years? I was in a little town with 600 people and no job opportunities."[2] ❞❞

When work usually meant hard physical labor, both men and women were worn out by the time they reached their 50s and 60s, so most didn't make it to retirement. But in today's digital age, more people use computers and phones and sit at desks in air-conditioned offices. Sophisticated machines do the heavy lifting. The idea of needing to rest at the end of your career because your body is physically worn out from long days of back-breaking work just isn't true for most people the way it was for past generations.

Along with the idea of retirement came the assumption that you "worked" until you "retired" from your full-time "occupation," "career," or "job." But today, the distinctions between working and retiring are blurring. The mandatory retirement age has been all but eliminated, and Congress has repealed the Social Security "earnings test" for people 65 or older. Government data show that the percentage of people over 65 who are in the workforce has been rising since the mid-1990s, after decades of declines. As of 2005, 13.8 percent of the 65+ population was in the workforce, a number that continues to increase.

Two contradictory trends are going on here. On the one hand, there's an outmoded societal attitude that people of a "certain age" should retire and, on the other hand, the facts show that these same people are staying active longer and longer in the workforce. Obviously, someone's hiring them!

Retirement is associated with other old-fashioned ideas about the people who retire: retired people can't be useful, they need to rest, they want to relax, they can't learn new skills. Nothing could be further from the truth!

Prepare for Stress

The transition to retirement is stressful, and that stress is made worse by not having a plan. The old adage "if you fail to plan, then plan to fail" is as true for retirement as for anything else. People who retire, leave stimulation behind, and don't replace it create stress for themselves. Leaving full-time work is a time of change, ambiguity, and lack of structure. It's easier to know where you're going if you begin to develop a road map ahead of time. That way, you can avoid the feeling of being out of control, which only leads to more stress.

Management gurus Peter Drucker and Peter Senge were familiar with the difficulties people face when they retire.[3] Drucker argued that many executives are simply "unprepared" for retirement. Other retirement experts agree. "We plan our careers, but we don't plan our retirement," says Dr. Phyllis Moen, director of the Cornell Employment and Family Careers Institute at Cornell University, who has studied couples' retirement transitions.[4] Dr. Moen's study substantiates a turbulent transition after quitting work. She found that for many couples, the first two years after leaving a job were a period of marital strife.

Taking Stock

Do you think you'll find not working stressful? We asked our friend, Dr. Tessa Albert Warschaw, noted executive coach, psychotherapist, author, and expert on resiliency, to address the issue of stress in the transition to retirement. Tessa reports that three main areas cause stress:

⇒ The lack of psychological preparation

⇒ The lack of fulfilling activities

⇒ The change in family dynamics

Tessa has created, especially for this book, the following questions to help you assess where you are in your preparation for the transition to retirement. Answer these questions and count the number of "yes" answers to see how you scored.

Taking Stock Quiz

I. Preparation:

1. Have you thought about restructuring or reinventing yourself? Yes / No

2. Have you spent time asking yourself *What's next?* Yes / No

3. Are you aware of the loss you may feel (e.g., loss of position, power, the game, the deal, a place to go, schedule, agenda, assistants, secretary, etc.)? Yes / No

4. Have you considered whether you'll miss the travel and entertainment perks of your job? Yes / No

5. Have you thought about how you'll feel about doing your own paperwork? Yes / No

6. Have you considered how you'll feel about not having a career purpose? Yes / No

7. Have you thought about whether you'll miss all those problems to solve? Yes / No

8. Have you anticipated whether you'll miss the triumphs and approvals? Yes / No

9. Have you considered whether you'll miss your title? Yes / No

10. Have you thought about whether your spouse will miss your title? Yes / No

Scoring for Part I:

Ten "yes" answers: Either of these two interpretations is possible: (1) You are well on the road to a smooth transition. You've thought through the main issues to prepare for the changes in your day-to-day life and are aware of the need to create "bliss" or internal fulfillment; or (2) you are in deep denial. You haven't come to grips with any of the changes about to take place in your life.

Seven to nine "yes" answers: You've done a lot of the preparation. Take a deeper look to see if it is, indeed, denial or just a few things you need to rethink.

Four to six "yes" answers: You're only about halfway. It's time for the SRR approach—Stop! Reflect! Review your "no" answers individually.

Three or fewer "yes" answers: You still have a way to go. You may have prepared for the pragmatic parts of your new life, but you still have to come to grips with the psychological issues. You'll meet troubled waters if you don't make some time for reflection and specific action.

II. Fulfillment:

1. Can you imagine going to a movie in the middle of the afternoon? Yes / No

2. Have you created an agenda for filling your time with avocations, interests, and worthy commitments of *your* choosing? Yes / No

3. Can you imagine, post-retirement, arising to face the day with the same anticipation you experienced during your career? Yes / No

4. Have you asked yourself, *If I knew I couldn't fail, what would I do next?* Yes / No

5. Have you drawn up a list of 10 things you always wanted to do in this lifetime? Yes / No

6. Have you remembered to include "play time" or making "play dates" not synonymous with golf or tennis? Yes / No

7. Do you feel you have life ambitions you want to fulfill? Yes / No

8. Do you think there's time to live your dream (if not now, when)? And do you have the desire to do so? Yes / No

9. Can you reconnect with those people in your past who brought you joy and appreciation for your friendship? Yes / No

10. Are you prepared to seek the truth, that you are more than your work? Yes / No

Scoring for Part II:

Ten "yes" answers: You are ready to go! Run with your ideas. You have a good start on creating a fulfilling future.

Seven to nine "yes" answers: You have a good sense of self, and you're ready to chart a course. Don't let dream stealers get in the way.

Four to six "yes" answers: You've probably been too busy to think about fulfillment. Find someone to talk to—coach, therapist, or another person. Now is the time.

One to three "yes" answers: Stop and rethink whether you are really doing what you *want* to do or what you *have* to do.

Zero "yes" answers: You must go beyond talking to someone and get into action. Inaction is the road to hopelessness.

III. Family Dynamics

Dr. Warschaw advises that the family dynamic can have a major impact on your retirement. Answer the following questions on family dynamics yourself and then have each family member answer them separately. Compare and discuss your answers together.

1. Will your partner miss your title?
2. Have you considered the changes in your family dynamic?
3. Will your being home more affect your partner?
4. Will your family see you as less powerful?
5. Will you consider yourself less powerful?
6. Will you transfer your "work style" to your home?
7. Do you see yourself setting up a command post at home—issuing directives, responsibilities, and orders?
8. Do you see yourself taking on household responsibilities (laundry, picking up cleaning, groceries, running family errands, cooking, etc.)?
9. Do you see yourself assisting younger family members or "baby-sitting" the grandchildren or elder parents?
10. Will you feel resentment for your partner who has not retired and continues to work inside and/or outside the home?

After your discussion, several things could occur:

➡ You discover that you need to think through a few more of your family responsibilities.

➡ You find that you still have a lot of work to do with your partner and the rest of the family.

➡ You see that things won't simply "fall into place."

➡ You discover that a family meeting is in order and that you are definitely in trouble in this area!

➡ You call for help and get some counseling.

➡ You happily learn that you, your partner, and your children are in total sync.

Without preparation, you may not have the satisfaction you've always dreamed of. Renee, one of our Real People, retired impulsively and wasn't happy afterward. We give Renee's story here and, as we do after each Real People story, the lessons and observations gleaned from it.

Real People: Renee

Renee is 65 years old. She retired at age 60. She has always loved education and teaching. After many years in the classroom, she went back to school at night and got an advanced degree that led to a job in education administration. She enjoyed this position for several years, until a change in leadership came along that she didn't like. One day, when she'd had enough, she walked into the superintendent's office and handed in her resignation. Renee had, for all intents and purposes, suddenly retired.

 Real Quotes

The idea of a "leisure society" with whole blocks of people with nothing to do except enjoy themselves, is to me a vision of hell, not heaven.
—Charles Handy, best-selling business book author and consultant[5]

Renee's husband, Carl, was, understandably, caught completely by surprise. He was phasing into retirement slowly in his real estate practice, still working three days a week. Renee was disappointed that Carl wasn't able to spend more time with her. She had other interests but none that really engaged her. She was in a political group she felt so-so about. She belonged to a reading group but found it disappointing because its members gossiped more than they discussed books. She grew increasingly frustrated and anxious.

As she enters her fifth year of not working, Renee regrets her hasty decision. She sees now that she retired for the wrong reasons. She is envious of her husband, who, in the five years since Renee retired, has made a smooth transition to not working at all. Thinking she'll never find what she really wants to do by herself, she tags along with Carl, but even the most loving couples don't always want to be together, and this is causing tension between them.

Lessons and observations:

➡ Renee quit working because she was fed up with office politics.

➡ She retired impulsively.

➡ She didn't discuss her decision ahead of time with her spouse.

➡ She expected her spouse to fill the gap in her retirement.

➡ She didn't spend enough time planning and exploring her options.

Renee left unanswered the most important question: why do you retire? If she had taken the time to plan what she wanted to do, she would have been a lot happier in retirement.

Why do *you* want to retire?

Reducing the Stress of Retiring

If you're thinking about quitting, you can avoid the problems Renee faced because she hadn't thought things through:

Know why you want to retire. Determine whether you're quitting impulsively, on someone else's schedule, or on your own schedule. Are you leaving for fun and relaxation? Are you leaving in frustration? Are you being forced out? Why you're leaving has an impact on where you're going and how easy your transition will be.

Admit to yourself if you're considering retiring because you don't like your job. A bad boss, being burned out, office politics, and tough commutes are not necessarily reasons to quit working, but rather to change jobs.

Be honest with yourself. Sometimes people mistake their jobs for their lives. If your job has become your identity, acknowledge it. You need to be aware that this work/ego involvement will affect your life when you quit working.

Dealing with Boredom

Retirement can be just plain boring. Robert Eisenberg, featured in *People* magazine (June 4, 2001) as America's oldest living worker at 103 years old, quit working in 1970, when he was 72, but after about 10 years he found retirement dull. So at age 82, Eisenberg took a job overseeing production as a consultant at Zabin Industries in Los Angeles, a zipper manufacturer he had previously owned.

❝❝ Real Quotes

The day I came home from work and discovered that my recently retired husband had rearranged the kitchen drawers, I knew we had a problem.
—Susan, 58

Boredom was one of the biggest complaints we heard in our research, and not just from Type-A personalities or hard-charging executives. In our in-depth interviews, retirees returned over and over to the theme of meaningful work. They wanted to be engaged in activity that was meaningful, not just activity for activity's sake. Walt, one of our Real People, was bored with retirement until he rediscovered an old passion. Here's Walt's story and the lessons and observations learned.

Real People: Walt

Walt, now 61, quit work at 58 after spending his entire career in advertising, starting as a copywriter. In the first few months after he retired, he and his wife traveled. Then he read books he'd never had the chance to read. But after 18 months, he hit the skids. He was bored out of his mind.

We coached him to get out and meet people. At a party, he met the dean of a nearby community college, who offered him the chance to teach a beginners' writing class. He tried it for two semesters and quit. He didn't enjoy teaching beginners, but he was intrigued with the skills that went into writing.

Walt met a former colleague who invited him to a writer's roundtable lunch. There he ran into old friends, one of whom asked if he would do some freelance writing for a newsletter company. Walt's freelance work led to his being asked to teach a graduate writing class.

After his previous teaching experience, he was hesitant to accept at first, but he discovered to his surprise that he loved teaching at this more advanced level. These students were committed to their work, dedicated to becoming better writers. They respected Walt. Walt decided to continue to teach writing at the graduate level.

Writing was his old passion, the one that had gotten him started in the business in the first place. He hadn't realized that passion still burned in him.

Lessons and observations:

➡ Walt was bored with traditional retirement.

➡ He rediscovered an old interest—writing.

➡ Walt wanted to be valued by audiences that he valued.

➡ He created his own options by getting out and talking to people.

Walt was able to recover from his retirement "slump" pretty quickly and with no real harm done. But we can't help but ask: *Why did he have to go through that in the first place?*

Stopping the Things You Love

If retirement means you stop doing things you love, it won't be a happy experience. In our experience working with clients, people underestimate the things they like about their work.

These can be small and large things. For example, Samantha, a retired salesperson who had commuted an hour each way to work for 15 years, felt something was missing in her life after she retired. She soon realized what it was, and it was something small: Samantha was an avid jazz music fan, and during her commute, she would listen to jazz CDs in the car as a way to relax. She needed to continue listening. She bought a portable CD player and decided to listen to the CDs while she worked out for an hour three times a week at the gym. With a little fine-tuning, she was able to schedule back into her life what she was missing.

Other situations are more challenging and the problems bigger. Dr. Hill, a retired physician we know, has never replaced the fulfilling recognition he got from practicing medicine. Here's Dr. Hill's story.

Real People: Dr. Hill

John Hill is a warm, fun-loving, 75-year-old physician. He is revered in his community, where he is known as "Doc." Dr. Hill left health care because of the increasing insurance paperwork and HMO-controlled managed care. Looking back, he feels he lost his identity. "Now I do the grocery shopping hoping to run into old patients who treat me like a celebrity."

When he quit working at age 72, Dr. Hill volunteered at the local hospital, but it was hard for him to let go of the "I'm in charge" mentality. After several awkward situations in front of patients, he and the hospital parted ways. Next he tried volunteering as a physician at a local men's prison. The inmates didn't appreciate him. Frustrated, he resigned after only three months.

He thought about joining a medical practice, but felt he just wasn't up to it physically.

To keep busy, he holds a leadership position in his church and is on the board of the local symphony, but these activities aren't satisfying enough. He says his biggest regret is that he doesn't play golf. In the end, he wishes he had found a way to continue his practice.

Lessons and observations:

➡ Being a doctor is Dr. Hill's life and identity.

➡ He quit because he was frustrated with industry changes, not because he was tired of practicing medicine.

➡ Recognition from audiences he values is his "hot button."

➡ Leadership roles in extracurricular activities do not fill his void.

➡ He wants to do hands-on medical work, but he has picked groups that don't give him recognition.

➡ Dr. Hill's patients gave him his sense of identity.

Is there anything in Dr. Hill's story you can recognize? Will you miss the people side of your work? Do you want to be recognized? If so, by whom? Where will you find these people?

Real Quotes

I knew I'd made a mistake when one of my golf partners asked if Kosovo was below Myrtle Beach.
—Paul, 68, retired at 65

Where Do You Fit In?

So far, we've introduced you to three real people who found it stressful to retire. How will you find retirement? Boring? Stressful? When you leave work, will you be leaving behind things you love to do? Do you want to focus on leisure activities, or do you want to keep more of what you're doing now? Where do you fit in? For example, do you believe any *shoulds* about retirement? *I should relax, I should quit working completely, I should want what my neighbor wants, I should travel.* In our research, we found that people believe too many "shoulds" when it comes to retirement.

You've heard about retirees who flunked retirement. You've met Dan and Arlene, Renee, Walt, and Dr. Hill, all people who didn't get it right. Now it's time for you to start thinking about what you want from retirement. Start with the vision of retirement you already have. You may not realize it, but you do already have one. It's been in the back of your mind. It's a picture that's developed from seeing your parents or other relatives retire, from watching colleagues or neighbors, or from the media. Your vision of retirement is important to be aware of because it's your starting point, your foundation as you begin the *rewire* process.

To help you figure out what that vision is, we have supplied self-exploratory questions. There are no right or wrong answers—only yours. Take the time to reflect on each question. After the self-exploration, write down in your journal or on a piece of paper the first thing that comes to mind. As you continue to read this book, keep these ideas in mind.

Quiz

Self-Exploration

When you imagine being retired, what picture comes to mind?

What do you anticipate adding to your life when you retire?

What do you envision giving up when you retire?

Do you have ideas about what your retirement should be?

Imagine not retiring. What image comes to mind? Is it positive? Negative?

Whose retirements have you observed? Parents? Aunts or uncles? Friends?

What would you like to emulate or do differently from the retirements you've observed?

If you're still trying to figure out what your vision of retirement is, here are a range of thought-starter questions for you. If you could retire right now, what would you do? Is your image of retirement getting up late and reading the newspaper? Is it playing more tennis or being outdoors more? Do you feel excited about not having to get on the interstate at 7 A.M.? Will you look forward to stopping for coffee any time you like? Will you miss the social lunches at work? How have you learned what you know about retirement? When you think about continuing to work past 62 or 65, how do you feel? Do you care what other people think of your retirement? Have you seen your parents retire? If so, what was their retirement like? How do you want yours to be different? Do you carry "baggage" that retirement *should* be a certain way? Reflect on your answers.

In our research, we found a link between a person's desire to seek an alternative to retirement and the attitudes they held about retirement. People shared with us many of the reasons they flunked retirement and went on to rethink traditional retirement. The following list comes from our personal interviews with retirees.

The Top Ten Reasons Why People Flunk Retirement

1. Retired for the wrong reasons.
2. Didn't realize the emotional side of retiring.
3. Didn't know myself as well as I thought I did.
4. Didn't have a plan.
5. Expected retirement to evolve on its own.
6. Thought rest, leisure, and recreation would be enough.
7. Didn't stay connected with society.
8. Expected my partner to be my social life.
9. Didn't know what I was leaving behind.
10. Was overcome with boredom.

REWIREMENT®: The Alternative

By now, we hope we've convinced you that a traditional retire-ment isn't for everyone. And maybe we've gotten you thinking about whether you'll modify traditional retirement to make it work for you. In the rest of this chapter, we focus on the alterna-tive, *rewirement,* and why it makes so many people so happy.

Changing the word from *retirement* to *rewirement* is more than just changing the *t* to a *w.* We came up with the term *rewire* one day when we happened to be in a record store where Tony Bennett's CDs were on display. We marveled at how well this entertainer, who had his own TV show in the 1950s and won two Grammy awards in 1962, had now repositioned himself for the twenty-first-century MTV generation. We laughed and said, "He's wired for action!" At the same moment, we looked at each other and said in unison, "No, he's *re*wired for action!"

We realized the similarities between Tony Bennett and the retirees we had been interviewing. They were all still the same people with the same skills and interests, but they had now refo-cused their energy in new contexts—or in Tony Bennett's case, for a whole new audience. Changing the *t* in *retire* to a *w* in *rewire* represents a whole new way of approaching life, of staying vital, of using your strengths and abilities, your gifts. It's a way of stay-ing active in work related to your field, working at something new, doing what you love, or staying connected to what makes you special.

Is Being Rewired for You?

In our research, we found that pre-retirees differed when it came to their outlook and attitude toward retirement. There were four main categories of attitudes:

➡ Those who were excited and knew what they were getting into

➡ Those who were excited but had no idea what they were get-ting into

➡ Those who were panicked and had no idea how to get in control

➡ Those who were angry and not physically or mentally ready but being forced into it

All but the fourth category of pre-retiree—those who were angry and not physically or mentally ready for retirement but were being forced into it—were open to the rewiring process.

We discuss rewiring in depth in Chapter 2, but for now we'll simply say rewiring is an alternative to traditional retirement because it encompasses activities that provide meaning, not just leisure. It includes expanded work options and opportunities to contribute to those around you by re-routing the energy that was spent in your prior occupation into flexible, satisfying retirement work opportunities—including full-time, part-time, flex-time, phased, sabbatical, seasonal, paid, personal, and/or volunteer. *Being rewired* is a customized, individualized way to live and work, one that may require a journey of discovery. It's for you if you are open to it.

How will you know if being rewired is for you? We developed the following list of attributes from the rewirees we talked to in our research. How many of the issues strike a chord with you?

The Top Ten Reasons to REWIRE™

1. Need mental stimulation.
2. Desire to do something meaningful, significant.
3. Want to do activities I've postponed.
4. Seek a balance between work and play
5. Want to continue to make money, but doing something I love.
6. Hope for a chance to turn an avocation into a vocation.
7. Want to stay physically and mentally healthy.
8. Desire to remain productive.
9. Hope to make a difference for others.
10. Need to stay connected.

Four Real Pre-Retirees

So far, we've seen that traditional retirement isn't for everyone. Now we'd like to introduce you to four pre-retirees who knew they wouldn't be happy with traditional retirement: Tom, Paula, Bob, and Carol.

As we first meet them here, they are beginning to think about retirement. We meet them again in Chapter 4 and in subsequent chapters, and we follow their stories as they evolve throughout the book. We track their progress as they follow the five-step *rewire* process. For now, Tom, Paula, Bob, and Carol know that traditional retirement isn't for them and they're beginning to envision what they want as an alternative.

The rest of this book describes in detail the rewiring process, shows you what it is all about, and gives you the steps to take to achieve it.

Real People: Tom

Tom, 58, has spent his career in sales and is now the national sales manager for a northwest-based technology company. He is the life of most parties. But he's burned out at work. The thrill of putting together winning sales teams and being on the road so much is beginning to wear thin. But the pleasure in developing salespeople and sales teams is more than just professional for him.

Tom broached with the division president the possibility of starting a "stepping-down" initiative, one in which he would begin to give up some of the travel and focus on developing a strong succession plan. But despite his good standing, Tom was told that the company had no mechanism in place to allow such a unique structure to occur. "You are either our national sales manager or you aren't," the division president said.

Tom is about to decide that he has earned his retirement, and although it will be tight financially, he is going to go for it. He has agreed to stay for at least six months, a year maximum, to get staffing right and to close pending deals.

Golf is his passion. Tom is in denial that he'll miss anything about work. He thinks golf, golf, and more golf will be enough for him as his retirement goal. His wife is concerned about whether golf alone will do it for Tom long-term. He used to coach his sons' Little League teams and thinks he could do something like that again. His wife is concerned about what he will do in the winter months when the course is closed and it's not baseball season.

Real People: Paula

Paula, a human resources executive, is in her mid-60s and has retired twice. Divorced, she has a 25-year-old daughter. Paula was a foster child and is a strong supporter of women's and young girls' issues.

Paula's first retirement was from a publishing company where she had worked for 25 years. She was 49. After six months, she decided what she had really needed was a sabbatical, not retirement. She realized that work had been her primary intellectual stimulation, and she missed the problem-solving.

She landed a position running the human resources department of a consulting firm. For seven and a half years, Paula thrived. She spoke at industry functions, sat on panels, and was quoted frequently in the media. But by the time she had reached age 57, Paula was tired. She retired for the second time.

Paula discovered sailing when she and her daughter went on a sailing vacation. After that, she took an intensive sailing course in Annapolis, Maryland. Paula then met a group of experienced sailors who asked if she wanted to crew on the Newport–Bermuda–St. Martin race. Paula, a quick study, knew she could meet this challenge and accepted. She spent a year as part of the team, and when she returned, she couldn't wait to go again.

When Paula was 59, her daughter asked her to consult on some human resources issues at the small start-up technology company where she was working. Paula created and implemented across-the-board policies and procedures that increased retention and made a positive impact on time to market and profitability. She joined the company as head of the human resources department.

Paula stayed 18 months and then started her own human resources outsourcing/consulting business, having seen the great need for those services in the growing technology field. She has crafted a niche business targeted to new technology and family-owned businesses.

Paula would like to cut back, but she doesn't know how to maintain her identity, sail, give back, and pull back at the same time. Having "retired completely" twice before, she doesn't want to do it again.

Real People: Bob

Bob is a 60-year-old senior engineer at an automotive company. He is an organization man in the best sense. He lives by the golden rule and thinks of the people in the company as his extended family. Because he continues to learn the new technologies, other engineers trust him as a problem-solver and think of him as the go-to guy for complicated technical problems.

Although Bob has had many promotions through the years, he is not a high-powered executive, just an extremely able and committed one. He is skilled at bringing different kinds of people together as a team. Bob, a World War I history buff, has a knack for rallying the troops around a mission—a skill management has recognized, especially during difficult times and waves of downsizing.

Long ago, his company recognized his give-back nature and put him in charge of the corporate United Way initiative. He was also selected to be its Junior Achievement spokesperson and to sit on the company's diversity council. Bob loves such assignments because (1) the recognition is great; (2) the company pays for his participation; and (3) his wife, especially, enjoys socializing with interesting celebrities.

Bob is nervous about quitting work for good. He has seen both work and church friends do it the right way and the wrong way. He would like to work part-time and is willing to forgo management responsibility if the company will consider a "phased" role for him. Bob would like to keep business and charity events in his life and nurture the community outside of the company. He would also like to work to earn money. The volatility of the stock market concerns him.

Real People: Carol

Carol, 51, fell into Wall Street, she didn't choose it. Even though she did well financially as an investment banker, she never believed that her purpose in life was to make other people rich. Carol has a wide network through her work in finance and from her after-hours work supporting politicians and fund-raising for their campaigns. She enjoys being a catalyst for change as well as having access to people from different walks of life.

At home, Carol loves to spend time with her journalist husband and her four English Setters. When one of them died unexpectedly, Carol honored his memory with a donation to the city's Center for Animal Care and Control. When she learned how many of the animals there would be put down, she decided to make saving animals her purpose in life. Carol adopted four dogs and took them to her vet to clean, fatten up, and board until she could get them adopted, either on her own or through a pet store.

Carol thinks that in saving animals she has found what she has lacked all along. This dream feels so close she can almost touch it.

You'll meet these four pre-retirees—Tom, Paula, Bob, and Carol—again in Chapter 4 and through later chapters in the book. We track their progress throughout the book as they *rewire* and you can see how their lives are transformed by the *rewire* process.

Don't Covet Your Neighbor's Retirement

By now, from meeting all the people we've introduced in the book—the retirees who were less than satisfied and the pre-retirees who are beginning to shape the nontraditional kind of retirement that will be more satisfying to them—you know that retiring is an individual process. One size does not fit all.

Tip

One size doesn't fit all. Don't covet your neighbor's plans. Seek advice, but remember that one man's meat is another man's poison. What works for your neighbor might not be right for you. Choice is the name of the game.

One day at lunch we overheard a conversation that made us laugh, but also made us realize how important it is to have a customized plan that's *yours:*

"Have you thought about what you're going to do in retirement?"

"Fishing, fishing, and more fishing!"

"Don't you think that'll get a little boring?"

"Not the way I've planned it."

"You've got a plan?"

"Sure. My wife loves the water. She is going to take sailing lessons, and we're even looking at property on a lake. We're going to structure vacations around fishing and try to fish in some of the great fishing spots in the United States. We've set some goals for ourselves. I was even thinking of writing an article for a fishing magazine. Remember, I *am* a journalist!"

"Maybe I better talk to my wife about taking up fishing."

"But you hate fishing!"

"I can learn to like it. You've done all the work; I'll follow your plan."

"What if I was a skydiver?"

In the next chapter, we talk about rewiring as a going *to*. In the meantime, we know from successful rewirees that it's never too soon to start planning. What steps have you taken to think about what you'll do in the next exciting stage of your life?

It's Never Too Soon to Plan

Have you begun to plan the lifestyle side of your retirement?

What do you get from work (not including money)?

What aspects of work will you miss (not including money)?

How will you replace the things you'll miss?

How strong is your personal network?

Chapter 2
REWIRING™ Your Energy

I blew the first half of my life, so I'm going for an Oscar in the second.

—*Jim, age 54, retired pilot*

Now that you're ready for the exciting journey of rewiring, you're ready to see the opportunity: rewiring is a going *to*. Rewiring is a proven alternative to traditional retirement—and we have the process and the research to back it up. In this chapter, we lay out the basics of rewiring, tell you what it means to *rewire*, and give you a sense of how you can go about it.

What Is *REWIRING*™?

First, the big picture. Rewiring is all about your personal energy flow; where you want it to go; and how using it will fulfill your mind, body, and soul. Rewiring starts with your physical and mental energy flow because it's wired into your body for life. You see, just because you turn out the light in your office for the last time, your energy doesn't stop flowing. The energy you used to spend in your work has to go somewhere. It needs to be rewired, or rerouted. This personal energy flow is a part of you, and it doesn't "retire" when you do.

Rewiring is the process of taking this energy and rerouting it into more satisfying alternatives. Rewiring is plugging in, turning on, flowing, and going! People don't retire, they *REWIRE*™.

How do people *rewire?* By taking the energy they used to spend on their full-time work and rerouting it into deeply satisfying, personally customized work activities (full-time, part-time, flex-time, phased, sabbatical, seasonal, paid, personal, and/or volunteer). Rewiring is the alternative to traditional retirement, with its emphasis on leisure-only activities. When people *rewire,* they create their own *rewire* options by customizing them from their deepest, most personal needs, or drivers, which we discuss in Chapters 3 and 4.

There are as many different *rewire* options as there are re-wirees, because rewiring is a personal choice. It's based on what you *want* to do or be, not on what you *have* to do or be. As we said in Chapter 1, forget about the shoulds. This time is for *you.* This is your chance to create a great next act. Why not make the most of it?

Tip

Rewiring is the process of rerouting personal energy that was spent in one's prior occupation into deeply satisfying, personally customized work activities including full-time, part-time, flex-time, phased, sabbatical, seasonal, paid, personal, and/or volunteer.

REWIRING™ Is All About *You*

Rewiring is different from retirement because it starts from inside you. Rewiring is different from other transition buzzwords and fads. It's different from reinventing, which is about changing yourself to fit into another career or job. It's also not about fixing something in your work life that isn't working, or fixing something that's wrong with your career or job. Changes like that are external. Rewiring is also different from just getting another job, even at retirement. Rewiring isn't about what's out *there* in the marketplace. Over the years, you've had to worry enough about that. This is about what's inside of *you.*

There's one source for everything that has to do with rewir-ing: *you.* Everything that has to do with rewiring comes from you, your personal motivators, your vision, your dreams, your goals, and your values. That's why rewiring is so satisfying for so many people.

The New Trend: Being Employed in a "Third Way"

If you receive a pension or Social Security and work for pay at the same time, you're part of a new trend, something we refer to as being employed in a "third way." Being employed in a third way refers to participants in the paid workforce who work and receive retirement income at the same time. "Working in retirement" used to be an oxymoron. Think about it. The two categories—"active in the workforce" and "receiving Social Security"—used to be thought of as mutually exclusive (and so the government used to limit the earnings of Social Security recipients age 65 and up). Now the two categories overlap to create a third category—"working retirees" or "retirees who work." The phrase "working retirees" isn't an oxymoron anymore!

Getting rewired is internally driven. You're the originator of the rewiring process—it's about listening to yourself and your own answers. Remember, the energy comes from inside you. Rewiring is not about responding to someone else's goals for you or living out society's agenda for you. At this point, you shouldn't listen to those old tapes. Rewiring is not about meeting your prior obligations. Now that you've paid down the mortgage, raised the kids, and done what you have to do, the question is what do you want to do now that you have the time and the freedom?

The Five W's of *REWIRING*™

What are the five W's of rewiring? They're the what, why, who, when, and where of rewiring. Here's an overview:

What? This has two parts, the first mental and the second physical. The mental part is to reroute your energy in the best way to meet your needs. The physical part is to decide the contexts and places in which you'll *rewire* and the people with whom you'll *rewire*.

Why? Society's changes force us to think differently and redefine retirement. We discuss the deep structural and psychographic trends supporting rewiring, including living longer and being healthier.

Who? Anyone who can consider traditional retirement can *rewire.* All you have to do is want it.

When? Rewiring can be done at any time and, as we said in Chapter 1, it's never too soon to plan to *rewire.*

Where? Every person rewires in his or her own way because rewiring is all about what works for you. *Rewirements* are as individual as thumbprints; no two are alike. We have worked with many different people who have followed the same five-step *rewire* process, and they have all come up with entirely different *rewire* outcomes. We give you examples to get your brain stimulated.

Now for an in-depth look at the five W's of rewiring.

The First W of REWIRING™: What?

Rewiring has both a mental and a physical component. The mental component is "getting your act together," and the physical component is "taking it on the road." Getting your act together entails defining where you want your energy to flow and go. This step requires looking inside to your deepest needs and can be difficult because many people have never taken the time to figure out what they want. Identifying your personal motivators, or drivers, is the key to figuring out where you want your rewired energy to flow. We give complete guidance on this important step in Chapters 3 and 4.

The second part, taking your act on the road, is the physical part. It refers to the decisions you have to make about where you will *rewire,* what kind of work situation you're looking for, the degree of commitment you want to make there, and what sorts of people you want to *rewire* with. We cover these issues in depth in Chapters 7 through 11.

Experimentation is an important part of taking your act on the road. It's important to get out and try things because things often turn out differently from what's expected. At 54, Robert took an early retirement package from the Gillette Corporation, planning to play more tennis and do more skiing and mountain biking. But he found that having fun full-time was boring. He readily admits that things turned out differently from what he first expected. "What I'm doing now is not precisely what I'd envisioned eight years ago," he says eight years later at age 62. "I have a three-part life—sports, charity work, and being an investment angel for fledgling start-ups."[1] It's not always easy to envision where you want to go.

Tip

Try experimentation. The process of exploring new things, or "trying different things on for size," is an important part of the *rewire* process. The rewirees we worked with were flexible and open. They tried new and different work options over a period of time to see what worked best for them. If they tried something and they didn't like it, they moved on, using what they learned to make a better selection the next time.

The Second W of *REWIRING*™: Why?

Some long-term societal and psychographic trends support rewiring. As you think about your life going forward, have you taken the following trends into account?

World-class longevity. If the American Association of Retired Persons (AARP) is right, scientists may be on the way to finding the fountain of youth. An article in *My Generation* describes how scientists are trying to alter the mechanism of aging itself. It argues that with the progress being made in bioengineering, if you are 50 today, you could live to have your pocket picked in 2083. (We can't help but add that if you want to have your pocket picked in 2083, you'd better save a lot of money so there's something left to pick!) In the next two or three decades, these scientific discoveries may significantly increase the average life span by as much as 10 or 20 years.[2] If the scientists are right, you could live to be 126 years old.

Europeans, who are less hung up about age than Americans, use the concept that there are four ages in one's lifetime: the first age for learning, the second age for work, the third age for living, and the fourth age for aging.[3] The metaphor isn't perfect, as there's overlap among the ages, but if you think of each age being 25 years, the third age starts around age 50 and the fourth age starts around age 75. Gerontologists have now redefined their view of the fourth age and refer to it as having four stages:

65 to 74: Young old

75 to 85: Middle old

85 to 95: Old old

95+: Frail old

We're living longer, healthier lives. Will you be in one of these categories?[4]

➡ For people over the age of 65, the rate of disability is decreasing.[5]

➡ People over the age of 85 are the fastest-growing age group.

➡ Seventy thousand people are centenarians, and this number is increasing.

➡ Three million baby boomers are expected to live to be 100 years old.

Will you live to 85? 100? Have you tried to picture what you'll do with all that time and what others around you will do? As The Beatles song says, "Will you still need me ... when I'm 64?" How about 85? Or 100? "You can't use the models of your grandfather or your fathers and mothers," says Dr. James E. Birren, who founded the gerontology program at the University of Southern California in 1965 and is now associate director for the Center on Aging at UCLA. "They didn't have the gift of long life that we have."[6] We need new models.

❝ **Real Quotes**

Don't tell me I'm going to live to 125! That's like going to a bad movie three times.
—Phillip, age 57 ❞

It's not news that people are living longer. The luxury of a long life span is one of the last century's greatest achievements, one that is ours to enjoy and make the most of. Even without the scientific advances molecular scientists are working on now, we know that on the average, if you're a man you can expect to live 18 more years after the age of 65; if you're a woman, you can expect to live 22 more years.

If you think about it, 18 years is a generation, time enough for a child to be born, grow up, and mature into legal adulthood. Eighteen years is enough time to have a career. Or maybe even two. So if you have had a couple careers before retirement, you could have one after you quit working full-time that's as long as or longer than one of your pre-retirement careers.

A final word: good health is necessary for a rewired life. While there are no guarantees, evidence shows that if we follow simple health guidelines, we can add years to our lives on average. Here's the list:

➡ Not smoking
➡ Drinking in moderation and never driving when drinking
➡ Having regular medical check-ups
➡ Eating a balanced, low-fat diet
➡ Maintaining a healthy body weight
➡ Keeping blood pressure in a normal range
➡ Wearing a seat belt
➡ Removing handguns from the home
➡ Seeking treatment if symptoms of depression persist[7]

You know you want to *rewire*—are you maintaining your good health?

Blending. Working after retirement is part of a national trend we call blending. By blending we mean the lessening of the distinct boundary between work life and personal life at retirement age. As we said in Chapter 1, retirement used to mean a one-time event, the end of paid work. But increasingly, people are working in part-time situations and as consultants after retiring from their primary career jobs.

Blending reflects two larger employment trends: less-rigid boundaries between corporations and employees, and the shortening of full-time careers at major corporations. First, the boundary between corporations and employees is more flexible as there's less loyalty and companies employ more workers who are not full-time employees. Charles Handy, in his 1989 business best-seller *The Age of Unreason,* observes what he calls the "withering" of corporations and argues that because less than one quarter of the population will have full-time jobs inside any organization, work will increasingly be done outside of corporations by people who are not full-time employees.[8] Other leading business commentators have made similar arguments. Peter Drucker called this idea "the collapsible corporation," and William Bridges has referred to this trend as the "de-jobbing" of the career.

The second trend is that corporate careers are shorter. Handy further argues that whereas in the past careers lasted 100,000 hours (approximately 50 years), corporations increasingly utilize 50,000 hours (approximately 25 years) of high-demand, high-stress work from "core workers" in their 20s, 30s, and 40s, a trend he describes as "half the people paid double, working twice as hard, and producing three times as much."[9] He argues that as they age, these highest-paid core workers will need to transition from being employed 24/7 inside corporations to being employed outside major corporations for the last third of their lives, as age discrimination, market competitiveness, or just plain hardheaded business realities dictate that a new generation will be asked to step up to the plate.

The bright side is that rewirees who want to work for pay have the opportunity to remain in the paid workforce on a flexible basis in phased retirements, as part-time employees, freelancers, consultants, or outside contract workers. As Handy argues, "There is going to be a lot of space for all of us, some-time, outside the formal jobs, especially since we are all going to live longer."[10] And the statistics at this point seem to back this up. Reversing a decades-long trend, Americans are retiring later in life. One out of seven people over the age of 65 was in the work-force in 2005.[11]

Rather than having an abrupt end to their work life at retire-ment, many people are looking for a way to gradually shift gears and pace themselves from working for a company full-time to other ways to be productive. As we show you later in the book, there are four ways to do this:

➡ Work for wages. Work for wages includes such things as working part-time, flex-time, sabbatical, corporate board, or in a phased retirement.

➡ *Work for a fee.* Paid work that includes working as a consul-tant for a fee, or working for yourself.

➡ *Work for me.* Some people also want a third kind of work that's intended to be pleasurable, even if purposeful, includ-ing learning something new. Purposeful learning is, after all, a kind of work, and includes such things as taking up a new skill, hobby, or language or getting training or certification.

➡ Work for free. This is work you give away, such as volunteer work, charity work, helping neighbors, taking care of family and friends, and home management work such as garden-ing, cooking, and other chores.

We give complete guidance on how to use these four catego-ries to create your rewired life in Chapters 9 and 10.

Because of the longer life span, people increasingly pursue "retirement careers" (another phrase that used to be an oxymoron but isn't any longer) and many other kinds of interesting work options. For example, Edmund Aleks, 59, found a way to balance a post-retirement career with his desire to spend more time with his son. After leaving the Los Angeles District Attorney's office with a nice pension, he now runs his own private investigative service and has the time to talk regularly with his son, a third-year resident in anesthesiology in San Francisco. He says, "I don't think any father in the world thinks he spends enough time with a son or daughter."[12] "Working in retirement" used to be an oxymoron because no one did it. Now, people are working in retirement, and the term we use has evolved into "working retirements." People don't retire, they *rewire*.

" Real Quotes

What is retirement? A liberation from mandatory duties.
—Jimmy Carter[13]

Demographics. Believe us. Although it may sound abstract, demographics have a big impact on you personally and on how you *rewire*, for one simple reason: when you reach age 62, the most popular retirement age, you will have *lots* of company. Whereas today there are 36 million people age 65 and over (12 percent of the population), in 2030 there will be a whopping 70 million people (20 percent of the population) in this age bracket. The fact that one out of five healthy, energetic people will be in his or her sixties means that society will have to catch on. This population "bubble," if it continues to flex its muscle to make things happen, is bound to make *rewire* options even more available and popular.

Recent statistics show an increase in the number of people age 65 and up in the workforce, with many getting *new* jobs.[14] Baby boomers are expected to expand on this trend and stay active in the workplace. If the 80 percent of the baby boomers who say they want to work in retirement end up doing so, the effect on the workplace will be staggering, with unprecedented numbers of people working after age 65.

Through their sheer numbers, baby boomers are taking the apparent contradiction of working in retirement and synthesizing it into a new mantra, the same way they did with *working mother, power yoga,* and *sports utility vehicle.* Baby boomers, as they have done so many times in the past, are moving beyond the either/or dichotomy to create a new groove. The current trend seems to indicate that many baby boomers will be working boomers when they retire.

Right now, rewiring is new. But we predict it won't be for long.

Psychographics. The rewirees we interviewed told us they wanted to work because it was a way for them to be connected to something larger than themselves and to find meaning. They thought traditional retirement, with its emphasis on leisure only, wasn't sufficient. Experts agree that the psychographics of retirement are changing. "For a long time, people were content just to be busy, but now people are looking beyond activity for activity's sake," says Marc Freedman, president of Civic Ventures, a San Francisco–based organization dedicated to mobilizing the time and talent of older adults for social service, and founder of Experience Corps, an organization that enlists volunteers 55 and up and sends them into schools in low-income urban centers to be mentors, tutors, and fund-raisers.[15]

Another reason people *rewire* is to enlarge their world by getting involved in projects that stimulate them intellectually and satisfy their curiosity, and in which they learn something new. In addition, we expect baby boomer rewirees to continue to want what they've always wanted: to achieve their personal goals, to get the most out of everything they've ever done, to continue with their active lifestyle, and to continue to enjoy their pleasure-seeking.

Real Quotes

When I retire, I'll have the time to rediscover myself. I used to be a nice person.
—Dick, age 56

Many will also want to make a difference. Norma Collier, a 62-year-old marketing manager, wanted to make a difference. "Before I die," she said, "I want to do something to make the world a better place, and this is the time to do it—not when I'm really old and decrepit, but when I'm still active."[16]

The psychographics point to rewiring as a trend. Will you be on board?

The Third W of REWIRING™: Who?

Who can *rewire?* Anybody! From the entrepreneur to the corporate person, from the currently retired person to the baby boomer whose retirement is still a few years away. We've worked with people from all walks of life and helped them *rewire*. We give you examples of rewirees throughout this book and show you how they got the most from their transformed lives. If you're in any one of the categories we've just mentioned, you're a potential candidate to be rewired.

The Fourth W of REWIRING™: When?

It's never too soon to start to *rewire*. And we recommend that you not wait until you're into retirement. Start to think about it now. Karen, a magazine publisher, began to *rewire* by making inroads into the world of folk art three years before she planned to retire. Here's Karen's story.

Real People: Karen

Karen, now 63, retired at 60 from her career as publisher of a popular women's magazine. She and her husband are avid art collectors. At age 57, Karen looked forward and realized that when she quit working, she needed something for herself, something different. But what?

She decided to look back to her old interest and passion, folk art. She got involved in the folk art movement by asking a friend who was the editor of a folk art magazine to introduce her to people in that community, including the president of the local folk art museum's board.

Karen sat on committees, demonstrated her commitment, and was acknowledged by the professional staff as having good ideas about new artists and good suggestions for new acquisitions. In retirement, she has succeeded as president of the folk art museum, which has allowed her to become a spokesperson for the folk art movement and to be recognized globally. Others have sought her out, and she is now collecting for major collectors and consulting.

Lessons and observations:

➡ Karen started planning three years before retiring.

➡ Karen returned to an old interest, folk art.

➡ Her new career dovetails with a hobby she and her husband share, collecting art.

➡ Her future is enhanced by an old passion.

You want to make the most of your *rewire* journey. Why not start to think about it now?

The Fifth W of *REWIRING*™: Where?

You can *rewire* anywhere. The number of options is limitless. Remember, there's no one way to *rewire* because the *rewire* journey is a personal journey based on your deepest motivations and needs. We give just one example here to whet your appetite. Peter took a sabbatical instead of retiring and then returned to the accounting firm where he worked. Here's Peter's story with his accompanying lessons and observations.

Real People: Peter

Peter, 55, is a partner in an accounting firm. He always goes the extra mile and expects a lot from himself and others. A road warrior for the past several years, he has traveled nonstop to meet the ever-increasing demands of clients, and this lifestyle is beginning to take its toll on his health. He can be very hard on himself.

Peter was ready to call it quits and retire. His wife and his partners were concerned. His wife feared if he retired, he would drive her crazy from boredom. His partners didn't want to see him go. The partners had been throwing around the idea of offering sabbaticals, similar to what Apple Computer did many years ago. They convinced Peter to be a guinea pig for the firm and accept a sabbatical rather than retire. The firm recommended three months, but Peter decided it was six months or nothing. His partners gave in, reluctantly.

Peter began his sabbatical with a visit to the doctor for a physical (which he passed with flying colors) and then a trip to the Caribbean for two weeks—the first two-week vacation he'd taken in 24 years! In the first month, he joined a gym and took a creative writing course, something he had dreamed about since he was a kid and found deeply satisfying.

Although he had no intention of going back to work when he started the sabbatical, by the fourth month Peter was beginning to lose it. He realized he had given up more than the stress of his job. He had given up the hustle and bustle, the spark—he hadn't realized that his work gave him energy.

In the fifth month, he began to prepare for re-entry into the firm. But this time he made a pact with himself. He would keep up with the workouts, keep the job in perspective, and try to work only five days a week. He would also start thinking about how to prepare for a good retirement in the future.

He calls his sabbatical a mini–test market retirement and gives himself a C+.

Lessons and observations:

➡ It's too early for Peter to retire, but he needs to start to think about what he'll do when the time comes.

➡ Peter needs to make room for more in life than work.

➡ When the time comes, he may be a candidate for phased retirement.

Tip

Ask about sabbaticals. Start thinking about phased retirement, sabbaticals, or flex-time options. Although the idea is still in a pioneering stage, as a step before full retirement, many employers will consider transferring employees to jobs with reduced responsibilities, schedules, and pay. Investigate these opportunities at your organization.

The Rewired Mind-Set

By now we hope we've convinced you of the opportunity, which is step one in the rewiring process. Retirement is a going *from*. *Rewirement* is a going *to*. Even more, we hope we've convinced you to believe in the rewired difference. Changing the *t* in *retire* to a *w* in *rewire* is more than semantics. It's a whole new mind-set.

Ten Ingredients for a Successful Rewiring
1. A positive attitude
2. Good health
3. An awareness of the financial picture
4. An open mind
5. A desire to stay connected
6. Self-knowledge
7. Meaningful interests or a desire to discover them
8. Intellectual curiosity
9. A willingness to explore
10. Flexibility

We believe in the *rewire* mind-set because we've seen it in action countless times with the rewirees we've worked with. Believing that you are going *to* a new experience instead of going *from* an old experience opens doors to a journey of possibilities. Notice we didn't say it guarantees the possibilities. Although these attitudes can't guarantee you satisfying rewiring outcomes, without them, a satisfying *rewirement* will be nearly impossible to achieve.

The following table contains our view of the rewired mind-set with the differences in attitudes we've seen in our research. We've already discussed some of the attitudes, and a few of them will be discussed in later chapters. All told, we believe these eight characteristics comprise the key differences that set rewirees apart from traditional retirees. Do you have the rewired mind-set? Will you have what it takes to *rewire?* Check your attitudes against those of the rewirees. Where do you fit in? Do you have the winning attitudes to make it happen?

The *REWIRE*™ Mind-Set

	Retirees	Rewirees
1. View of the World of Work	It's about jobs	It's about customized work situations
2. Approach to social networks	Disengage or don't develop	Stay in touch and nurture
3. Attitude about intellectual stimulation	Job requirement	Lifelong interest
4. Purpose of self-knowledge	Why bother?	First step in finding fulfillment
5. Importance of skills	Not necessary	Can be important
6. Mental attitude	Accept the status quo	Optimistic that positive change is possible
7. Activity and health	Inactive lifestyle; passive about health	Active lifestyle; actively manage health
8. View of the future	Best is past	Best is yet to be

From our research, we found that these eight delineators define the rewired mind-set:

View of the world of work. Rewirees looked at work as a customized work situation, not a job. They didn't job hunt by typing "part-time job opportunities" in their search engines or looking in the classifieds in the newspaper. They didn't want the marketplace to determine what they would do. They wanted their dreams to determine what they would do, so they went out to create them. We discuss creating customized work options in Chapters 7 through 11.

Approach to social networks. Rewirees fed and nurtured their social networks and found a lot of their opportunities through contacts. They saw networks as opportunities to give, not just take, and invested their time, goodwill, and financial resources, if necessary, to feed and nurture friends, community groups, and other contacts. They didn't isolate themselves. The topic of personal networks and other resources are discussed in Chapter 12.

Attitude about intellectual stimulation. Rewirees viewed learning as a lifelong commitment, not just as something you do for a job. They were curious and inquisitive, read the newspaper to keep up, and asked lots of questions.

Purpose of self-knowledge. Rewirees viewed self-knowledge as critical to the process of figuring out how to live life to the fullest. Their self-knowledge provided the framework in which they made their choices, including knowing what they wanted to continue with and what they could drop. They used their self-knowledge to figure out what they got from work, to prioritize options, and to make choices. Self-knowledge helped them define the trade-offs and figure out how much time they were willing to commit to any particular activity before jumping in. The tool rewirees used to enhance their self-knowledge is the drivers, which we cover in Chapters 3 and 4.

Importance of skills. Rewirees viewed their skills as assets to nurture and develop. They expected they would have to learn things they didn't know how to do and were proactive about learning new skills. We talk about skills in Chapter 8.

Mental attitude. Rewirees had a positive mental outlook. They were optimistic and hopeful overall and didn't give up when they faced obstacles. As one man said to us about his successful *rewire* journey, "I learned not to be a quick quitter."

Activity and health. Rewirees were active physically on a regular basis. They walked, exercised on a stationary bike, or pursued other activities often. They actively managed their health, had regular checkups, and followed medical advice. They didn't smoke, didn't abuse alcohol or drugs, ate moderately, and kept their weight in a healthy range. Believe us, we're not saying rewirees are saints, but they know that without good health, it's difficult to have the personal energy to *rewire*.

View of the future. Rewirees believed that the best is yet to be. They structured a life in which they found satisfaction in each day and looked forward to getting up in the morning.

In our research, we asked rewirees, "What would you advise those who are starting out on this process?" The list of their pointers follows.

The Top Ten Pointers from People Who Have Rewired
1. Have a plan.
2. Plan to evolve.
3. Test-market ideas.
4. Dare to discard.
5. Recognize goals can change.
6. Learn from others.
7. Don't look to others for direction or approval.
8. Think of freedom as a good thing.
9. Think of too much freedom as a bad thing.
10. Don't overcommit.

Rewirees also added their number-one piece of advice: know yourself. The issue is not whether there will be opportunities; the challenge will be for you to discover or create them. The key is how to figure out what motivates you.

The way to know this is to know your drivers. Identifying your drivers is step two in the *rewire* process. In the next chapter, we introduce this step and show you how drivers are the key to customizing your own personal brand of satisfaction. In Chapter 3, we begin to answer the following questions. Have you thought about them?

➡ How well do you think you know yourself?

➡ Can you list the top three things that drive you to select the kind of work you do?

➡ What motivates you to work (besides money)?

Step II
Identifying Your Drivers

Chapter 3
Your Drivers: Why You *Really* Work

Why do I work? I love the glamour and excitement of TV.
—Lily, age 49, sitcom writer

Now that you know you have rewired energy, what will you do with that energy? How will you figure out what will give you the most satisfaction in your rewired life? The key to finding the answer is to look inside yourself. The key is your *drivers*.

One of the most important parts of the entire rewiring process is for you to become aware of your personal motivators, or drivers. Knowing what you get out of work helps you select future activities that will be most satisfying and fulfilling to you. In this chapter, we provide an overview of the drivers. In Chapter 4, we show you how to select your own drivers.

Identifying your drivers, step two in the *rewire* process, puts you in charge. No one else feels your drivers the way you do—not your spouse or even your best friend. Drivers make your rewiring uniquely yours because they help you look inside to discover what really turns *you* on … if you are honest with yourself.

What Are Drivers?

Drivers are personal motivators we use as a selection tool to choose how to match our deepest needs with the world around us. For example, when our friend Sam says "I love to win at business," he is expressing his competitive driver. Drivers are what make you tick as a human being because they go deep inside you, to your brain, heart, and ego. We all have drivers.

Our drivers are fairly consistent over our lifetime. For example, it's a safe bet that Sam, the man just mentioned with the competitive driver, may have liked to play competitive team sports as a kid. Our drivers don't change, but we make different choices about fulfilling them over our lives.

Remember how we said in Chapter 2 that when you retire, your energy doesn't stop flowing? That's because your drivers still drive you. The key lesson to remember about drivers is that they are part of your rewired energy. As with your rewired energy, your drivers don't go away just because you retire. Don't make the mistake many people do of thinking that you don't need to fulfill your drivers anymore. You do! Drivers stay with you, the same way your energy does, and remain an important part of your life. For example, to Frances, a senior financial executive, her company was like an extended family. The workplace fulfilled a deep need of hers, to belong to an organization—what we call her belonging driver. When she retired, she found a way to continue to meet that driver by volunteering at a large non-profit organization.

Real Quotes

I'll be glad to give up the rat race, but not all of the people who ran the race with me.
—Frank, 59

You Work for More Than Money, Honey!

We began to see the importance of drivers when, as executive search consultants, we worked with people who were looking for new jobs and careers. Our candidates were honest—sometimes brutally honest—about what they wanted in their careers besides money. Their openness first made us see the importance of drivers and inspired us to dig deeper into their significance in our original research with retirees and pre-retirees.

Drivers are the key to satisfaction. They enable you to match your deepest needs with your work, job, career, and other activities. Jack and Robin are two candidates we worked with whose honest assessment of their needs opened our eyes to the importance of drivers. We give their Real People stories in the following paragraphs. As you read them, look for clues about what Jack and Robin see as their needs from work, what motivates them to work, and what kind of payoff they get from work. Check your mental answers against the list of needs provided after each of their stories. Jack and Robin didn't use the word *drivers*, so we don't either. Instead, we refer to them as *needs*.

Real People: Jack

Jack, 47, is the vice president of marketing at a consumer packaged-goods company based in Chicago. He is a marketing wiz and, as he himself admits, he's bored. He's been at the company too long. In the beginning, the new products he launched attracted the attention of the top brass, but they don't now, as they're well established. For Jack, there are no high-pressure decisions and no adrenaline rush. The products are no longer interesting or stimulating to him. He wants an exciting new product to be passionate about. He also wants to go to a new company to be in a more stimulating corporate culture and to be in the center of the action. He also wants to have a large staff reporting to him—25 to 30 people. He is looking forward to the change and is willing to relocate his family to find an opportunity that really excites him and is a good career opportunity.

Jack's needs are …

➡ To be part of the action. Jack wants the adrenaline rush of high-risk new product launches.

➡ To be with intellectually stimulating people. Jack's bored with the company and the people he's working with now.

➡ To have power. He wants to have 25 to 30 people reporting to him.

➡ To pursue a passion. Jack wants to feel passionate about the products he's marketing.

Real People: Robin

Robin, 48, is a senior vice president of a pharmaceutical company. She is frustrated by the lack of team spirit in her organization. The company has had considerable turnover, and she is feeling disenfranchised. She recently lost some of her team to marketing when it was reorganized, and her leadership skills are not being used as they were before. Her sales division has beaten goals for the past three years. She would rather make money for another company that recognizes her leadership potential and appreciates her for the strong manager she is.

Robin's needs are ...

➡ To have a sense of belonging. Robin is frustrated by the lack of team spirit in her organization. She would rather work in a company where she can be part of an effective team.

➡ To be a leader. The new corporate organization doesn't use her excellent leadership skills.

➡ To have prestige. She wants to work for a top company with market-leading new drugs.

➡ To be recognized. She would rather work for a company that recognizes her leadership and management skills.

From Jack and Robin, you've seen eight different needs people satisfy through their work. But there are many other needs that are met from work. What do you get from your work (including paid and volunteer work)? Why are you in the line of work you're in? What do you get from your current job? We'll start to look at that in the next section.

Why Are You in Your Job?

As search consultants, we have a motto: *use your today to build your tomorrow*. In other words, before you jump ahead and imagine what your drivers will be in the future, look at what drives you in your life *today*. As we always say, if you know who you are today, you can build on who you want to be tomorrow.

Tip

As you start to focus on your drivers, you may find that your current job or career isn't fulfilling many of your drivers. If that's the case, hold on to those thoughts. As you continue to read this book, you'll find information useful in finding driver fulfillment.

As recruiters, we've found that people have a love/hate relationship with their work. What people initially run from often turns out to be what they run *to* once it's gone. Surprisingly, people don't spend much time thinking about the good things they get from work besides money. So we're going to spend a little time on this now. Why did you choose your work or career? What is it about the job you have that attracted you in the first place? What psychic rewards do you get out of it? What are the negatives and the positives? We'll start to answer these questions right now, although we won't ask you to actually identify your drivers yet—that comes in Chapter 4.

Let's start with your current job. How did you select it? Jot down your answers to this and other questions in the following quiz.

Quiz

How Did You Select Your Job?

What was the best job(s) you have ever had? Survey your entire career.

What made it the best job? List as many reasons as possible.

If you could rewrite your current job description, what would you throw out and what would you keep?

Did you plan your career? If so, how did you do it?

Or did your career just evolve? If so, how did it evolve?

Are you happy with your career (yes or no)?

Why or why not?

What career changes would you like to make?

What about your work gives/gave you meaning?

What makes you look forward to work each day?

This quiz may have been hard for some and easy for others. Trying to answer these questions can be both eye-opening and intimidating. For some of you, it may have shown that your career followed a complete road map. For others, it may have showed that your career had more of a dartboard mentality—you just got there. The key thing is that answering these questions may have raised some red flags, provided you with a personal alert or wake-up call, or pointed out some missed opportunities.

For example, there may be a reason why you loved a particular job. Why did you leave it? Maybe you sold medical equipment in the health-care field and then moved into selling computers because the money was better. But maybe you always missed something about the health-care field, something you never found again when you sold computers. Or maybe instead of the industry, it was the job itself or the function. That's an important piece of information you should know. Information like this gives you a clue where to look for fulfillment on your *rewire* journey. It's good to think about what you liked and didn't like in the past because it sheds light on your future possibilities.

Take a look again at what you answered in the preceding quiz. What reasons did you give for liking your job? Do any reasons jump out at you? Is there a pattern? What are you getting out of your job (besides money)? Have your career and job choices been for the right reasons or the wrong reasons? Were the choices you made really yours or did other pressures influence you? Have the rewards you get from your career changed over time?

Don't lose track of any of the ideas you came up with here. Your answers provide clues for opportunities down the road.

The List of Drivers

As executive recruiters interested in the lifestyle side of retirement, we made a connection between the use of drivers in matching job candidates and jobs and the use of drivers to find satisfaction in rewiring. It seemed obvious to us that, because drivers don't go away, they could also serve as the basis for finding satisfaction in the new alternative to retirement, *rewirement.*

In our research with retirees and pre-retirees, we asked them what they got out of their work besides money. We came up with a list of 85 drivers, listed in Appendix C at the back of the book. We then culled the list down to the 30 drivers retirees and pre-retirees most commonly told us were the reasons why they worked.

As we probed in one-on-one interviews with retirees, we realized that the happy people had either intuitively known what their drivers were and fulfilled them with new activities after they retired, or they discovered how to satisfy them through trial and error. Aha! We were onto something.

In fact, other studies show that the majority of retirees work for pleasure, mental stimulation, and personal fulfillment. One of the most important trends is for retirees to return to the working world. In the 2001 Cornell Retirement and Well-Being Study, 44 percent of retirees say they've worked for pay at some point after they've retired. The most popular reason for returning to work (89 percent) was to keep active, not financial need. Other reasons include the following:

➥ Have free time (73 percent)

➥ Desire additional income (63 percent)

➥ Not ready to retire (58 percent)

➥ Maintain professional contacts (56 percent)

➥ Maintain social contacts (56 percent)

➥ Need additional income (41 percent)

➥ Health insurance (10 percent)

Of those currently employed after retirement, 14 percent say they will "never retire" and 28 percent say they will work "as long as I am healthy." Most see that they have the chance for a "new chapter" in their lives and want the new experiences to match it. They want their work to be based on choice, personal passions, and interests.[1]

What are the reasons you work? Skim the following list of 30 drivers. Do any of the reasons people give for working sound familiar to you? If so, make a mental note of them for now.

The Thirty Drivers

The following drivers are listed in alphabetical order by the name of the activity (for example, *Accomplishments*) and then by how a person engages in the activity (to have accomplishments). They are not ranked by importance or popularity. Our research did not ask pre-retirees and retirees to rank their drivers, and we excluded money.

#1 Accomplishments—to have accomplishments

#2 Action—to be "part of the action"

#3 Authority—to be an authority figure

#4 Belonging—to have a sense of belonging

#5 Competition—to be competitive

#6 Creativity—to be creative

#7 Current—to be current or "in"

#8 Experiences—to have new experiences

#9 Friendship—to develop friendships

#10 Fulfillment—to be fulfilled

#11 Global—to have global opportunities

#12 Goals—to have and to share goals

#13 Identity—to have an identity

#14 Intellectual Stimulation—to be with intellectually stimulating people

#15 Leadership—to be a leader

#16 Lifelong Learning—to be constantly learning

#17 Making a Difference—to help make the world better

#18 Mentoring—to mentor others

#19 Passion—to pursue a passion

#20 People—to have exposure to people

#21 Power—to wield power

#22 Prestige—to gain prestige

#23 Problem-Solving—to be a problem-solver

#24 Recognition—to be recognized

#25 Self-Esteem—to enhance self-esteem

#26 Skills and Talent—to develop skills and talent

#27 Social—to be connected to others

#28 Structure—to have structure

#29 Value—to give value to others or to be valued

#30 Visibility—to have visibility

Drivers in Action

Now that you've skimmed the list of drivers and are beginning to get a feel for them, it's time to get an idea of how they work in people's lives. At this point, to illustrate how drivers work, we return to the Real People rewirees you met in Chapter 2, Karen and Peter.

First, Karen. Karen is the women's magazine publisher who chose folk art as her rewired career. As you'll recall, Karen had a passion for collecting folk art. While she worked at the magazine, collecting folk art was just a hobby. But when she rewired, she decided to turn her passion into a new career. She became active in a local folk art museum, eventually serving as president. Karen's rewired career met four drivers:

Driver #4: Belonging—to have a sense of belonging. Karen needs to have an organization around her, and she takes pride in belonging to an institution. She is not a stand-alone entrepreneurial person, and she knows it.

Driver #13: Identity—to have an identity. As you may recall, at age 57 and while still at the magazine, Karen started to think about what she would do when she retired. She knew she would need something "for her" after she retired. Reserving something "for herself" is Karen's way of saying that she needs activity to give her an identity.

Driver #19: Passion—to pursue a passion. Karen knows she is happiest when she is passionate about something. Folk art is her passion. She loved to collect it before she retired, and it made sense to pursue this passion for her rewired career.

Driver #24: Recognition—to be recognized. Recognition is important for Karen. Karen recommended new artists and new acquisitions for the folk art museum to purchase. It was important for Karen that the professional staff acknowledge her good taste in folk art and her leads on new artists.

Although Karen had a passion for folk art, she knew her drivers and knew that collecting art to fill her home would never fulfill her.

Now we'll discuss Peter, the second rewiree you met in Chapter 2. Peter is an accounting partner who, instead of quitting for good, took a six-month sabbatical. During the sabbatical, Peter took a creative writing class. He also woke up to the fact that he needed more balance in his life, but that without his work, his life had no pizzazz. Here are Peter's drivers:

Driver #1: Accomplishments—to have accomplishments. Peter is a rainmaker for his firm and takes great pride in winning new accounts.

Driver #2: Action—to be "part of the action." Peter likes being in the eye of the hurricane. He found during his sabbatical that he missed the hustle and bustle of his work. When he was out of the office, he felt he had left a part of his life behind.

Driver #6: Creativity—to be creative. Peter took a creative writing course on his sabbatical and felt deeply satisfied by it. He has an untapped creative side that's not being met at work.

Driver #12: Goals—to have and to share goals. Peter enjoys getting difficult tasks done. The more demanding the client or situation, the more fired up Peter gets.

Peter recognized that he needed to have more balance in his life and that he also couldn't or shouldn't make decisions based on current frustrations.

Drivers: The Keys to Satisfaction

Now that you've seen examples of how the drivers work in Karen's and Peter's lives, you may be asking yourself about what drivers are being met in your own life. If you ever find yourself saying at work, "I'm bored, I need to be challenged," now you know why. That message is from an untapped driver, and you'd better tune in!

As you've seen, drivers are important because they're selection tools that guide you to satisfaction. Ignore them at your peril as you embark on the *rewire* journey. Embrace them, and you'll be able to find the best and most satisfying choices from the world of choices. How does this journey of self-discovery begin? By identifying your drivers.

In the next chapter, we complete the second step of the *rewire* process: identifying your drivers. Knowing them is the key to life satisfaction when you *rewire*. Are you ready?

Chapter 4
Discovering Your Hidden Drivers

I love to negotiate, and I love to win. I thrive on the game of business.

—Mary, 48, lawyer

Many people don't realize what they get from work besides money. So when they reach retirement time, they don't know how to find fulfilling work or activities because they never identified what fulfills them in the first place.

In this chapter, you learn to identify your drivers, the things that turn you on and make you tick as a person. Knowing your drivers and then finding activities that fulfill them is the key to satisfaction. Our research shows that when people satisfied their drivers, they were happy in their retirement. In fact, driver satisfaction was more important than whether or not people got paid for their work.

The Benefits of Knowing Your Drivers

Knowing your drivers enables you to make choices—more efficiently than if you didn't know them—between different types of activities, organizations, and commitments. Your drivers give you a focal point for your *rewirement* planning by showing you where your emotional payoff, satisfaction, and fulfillment have come from in your life. They don't tell you what specific kinds of activities, jobs, or organizations you want to be involved with. It's your job to pick the activities you think will give you the best match between your drivers and the activities you're pursuing. We talk about selecting activities in Chapters 7 through 11.

We've seen many people who didn't know their drivers and ended up wasting precious time and energy doing something that wasn't right for them. Do you remember Dr. Hill, the physician you met in Chapter 1, who missed practicing medicine after he retired? All his post-retirement activities failed to fulfill him because they didn't satisfy his recognition driver. In contrast, Karen, the magazine publisher you met in Chapter 2, went on to find great fulfillment at the folk art museum because she knew it was important to her to have an identity, to belong, and to pursue a passion (three of her drivers). Karen intuitively knew what she needed to do to find satisfaction. In other words, she had identified her drivers. She knew what turned her on.

In this chapter, we show you how you can identify your drivers, walking you through this most important second step in the *rewire* process. It's a journey of self-discovery—and the most challenging work we ask you to do in this book—but we guarantee it's worth it!

Driver Assessment

We presented the list of the 30 drivers in Chapter 3. That might have gotten you thinking about what your drivers are. You might have a pretty good idea already, or you might be in the dark about what motivates you. Now is the time to focus intensely on your drivers. To help you pinpoint what your drivers are, we list the 30 drivers again in the later "First Pass" section, this time with assessment questions for you to ask yourself about each one. The questions describe behaviors that relate to the drivers to help you recognize what we mean by each driver and enable you to identify on your own what your particular drivers are.

Each assessment question gives a representative selection of behaviors that might characterize a particular driver. For example, under "to be an authority figure," the assessment questions are: Do you like to be regarded as having all the answers? Do you enjoy having people seek you out for advice and counsel? Do you like to be perceived as an expert on a specific topic?

We stress that the assessment questions are a representative selection, not an exhaustive list of behaviors relating to a particular driver. You might think of behaviors that could also apply to a particular driver, and that's okay. The point here is not to be exhaustive. The important point is to get you thinking so you can identify your drivers.

Drivers: Different Meanings for Different People

Before you can begin to identify your drivers, you're going to need some background on how drivers fit into people's lives. First of all, remember that the drivers aren't actions or activities. Drivers are motivators inside you—they're an integral part of you. You fulfill your drivers (which are internal) when you take part in activities (which are external).

Drivers mean different things for different people and fit into people's lives in very different ways. Therefore, when you read the list of drivers, you shouldn't get too hung up on the literal meaning of each assessment question. For one thing, people have their own individual lens or viewpoint through which they act on their drivers, consisting of their values, beliefs, and attitudes about what's important to them. For example, the social driver may mean organizing the golf tournament weekend for one person and attending Chamber of Commerce meetings for another. Individual differences mean that two people fulfill the same driver in completely different ways.

Identifying the driver is just the beginning, as a story from our work illustrates: as executive recruiters, we often work with candidates and ask them the reasons why they want to change jobs or careers. One day we got a call on referral from Cynthia, a woman looking for a new job.

"Jim says you are great at helping people find their ideal job," she said.

"Well, it doesn't exactly work like that," Jeri replied. "You need to know what you want."

"I'm tired of law," she said. "I've made a good living, but for me, work is more than money. I want to make a difference."

"What do you mean by making a difference?" Jeri asked. "Do you want to make a difference using your legal background? For example, to provide legal services for people who can't afford them? Do you want to establish a scholarship for low-income students who want to study law? Or do you want to make a difference in some other area besides law? That could be anything from creating a nonprofit to working in a soup kitchen. Perhaps we should explore what you mean by making a difference."

As this story shows, Cynthia was only at the beginning when she said she wanted to make a difference. Drivers are the place to start, but they need further interpretation to be most meaningful. (We cover this later in the book.) As you'll see, it's not enough to know you have a particular driver, because drivers mean different things to different people. Cynthia had some more exploring and thinking to do to find out what she meant by making a difference. To whom did she want to make a difference? Did she want to make a difference as a professional, or in a more personal way? After Jeri asked her the initial questions, we sat down and worked with her to come up with her own interpretation of her driver.

Real Quotes

The need to know that we are making a difference motivates doctors and medical researchers to spend hours looking through microscopes in the hope of finding cures for diseases. It drives inventors and entrepreneurs to stay up nights trying to find a better way of providing people with something they need. It causes artists, novelists, and composers to try to add to the store of beauty in the world by finding just the right color, the right word, the right note. And it leads ordinary people to buy six copies of the local paper because it has their name or picture in it.

—Harold Kushner, *Living a Life That Matters*[1]

Interpretations of Drivers

We hope the idea of how drivers fit into people's lives is beginning to be clearer to you. As you've seen, drivers need to be interpreted with your own personal spin to be meaningful in your life. The fact that people personalize the drivers in ways that are unique to their own personalities becomes clearer when we introduce two Real People, Chip and Mary, clients with whom we have worked. Their background stories aren't important here. Instead, what we want to focus on is the different meanings the drivers have for each of them.

Chip, a 50-year-old marketing executive who works at a bank, admits that working gives him ...

> Fulfillment (#10 Fulfillment—to be fulfilled).
>
> Global exposure (#11 Global—to have global opportunities).
>
> Leadership positioning (#15 Leadership—to be a leader).
>
> Recognition (#24 Recognition—to be recognized).
>
> Visibility within the bank and the community (#30 Visibility—to have visibility).

Mary, a 43-year-old graphic artist working for a design firm, says that working allows her to ...

> Be on the cutting edge (#7 Current—to be current or "in").
>
> Pursue her passion (#19 Passion—to pursue a passion).
>
> Use her gifts and talents (#26 Skills and Talent—to develop skills and talent).
>
> Mix in a desired social environment—for her it is other artists (#27 Social—to be connected to others).
>
> Have visibility (#30 Visibility—to have visibility).

As you probably noticed from the lists of Chip and Mary's drivers, both Chip and Mary share the visibility driver. But these two very different people mean two very different things by visibility. Here are the different interpretations Chip and Mary have for Driver #30 Visibility:

Chip likes the visibility he gets from his senior banking position because ...

➡ He is perceived as being slightly above his peers within the overall banking community, here in the States and worldwide.

➡ The visibility leads to respect, as clients and colleagues seek him out.

➡ He is often quoted in trade journals and is asked to speak at industry events.

➡ Headhunters know him.

For Chip, visibility means relative ranking among his peers and keeping his options open on the job market.

Mary likes the visibility she gets from her design position because ...

➡ Her boss and her peers perceive her as quite talented, and she's asked to do the company presentations to potential clients and investors.

➡ As she has gained seniority, she has had the chance to display her work outside the firm.

➡ She gets credit for her work in magazines and likes having a byline because it leads to freelance work outside the firm.

For Mary, visibility means her talent is recognized and leads to freelance opportunities.

As you've seen, drivers mean different things to different people. With this point in mind, you're now ready to go forward to the next section, which has advice on how to approach identifying your drivers.

Advice on Identifying Drivers

Now that you're getting ready to study the list of drivers and the accompanying assessment questions, it's important to offer a few words on how to approach the task of selecting your drivers. From our experience, we've found that for many people this sort of self-assessment is a first and can be a daunting and challenging task.

We hope this advice is helpful before you proceed:

Be honest. It takes candor and honesty to select accurate drivers, ones that are really you. This is not a beauty contest. "Own" the drivers you really have, and don't worry about those you don't.

Focus. Exclude, if you can, any behaviors or activities that come with your duties, obligations, or social pressures unless you really value and like them. You shouldn't consult with anyone else about your drivers, either. Don't ask other people what they think. Don't answer based on how you would like to see yourself or how you would like others to see you, but on how you really are. Before you pick a driver, ask yourself if it's really you.

Balance. In approaching the drivers and the assessment questions, think about your whole life—not just your most recent job. If you're having a bad day, come back and try again when you're feeling more balanced. A bad mood can distort your answers.

Reflect. Take time to reflect on your answers. Selecting drivers is *not* something you should do in one sitting. In our experience, some people need to go through the list three times to be able to identify their drivers.

The process of identifying drivers is not logical. It's an intuitive or "gut-feel" exercise. If you're still having trouble, review the tips for identifying drivers in the following box.

Troubleshooting Tips for Identifying Drivers

Immediately eliminate any driver that registers no importance at all.

Make more than one list, and compare the lists to see if they're the same or different.

Never say never. In other words, don't exclude any driver that registers with you just because you haven't had the time in your life up to now to act on it.

Think over the course of your whole life—professional and personal. Look at your resumé and think back over your career in five-year intervals, if that helps you. What drivers have you always fulfilled? Which ones have changed?

If you have a strong negative feeling about a particular driver, ask yourself if this is in reaction to your job. If it is, you may be overreacting.

First Pass

We recommend that you make more than one pass at reading through the list of drivers. Ideally, you should go through the list three times. If you're currently working, ask yourself *What drivers am I currently using at work?* If you're retired, think about the jobs you had prior to retirement. If you're having trouble, think back in five-year periods to all the different jobs (paid and unpaid) you've held. About each job, ask yourself, *What drivers was I fulfilling in that job?* Immediately ignore any driver that isn't you. Your goal is to try to select 5 to 10 drivers from the list of 30. After you've completed the first pass, put it down for a day or two if you need to. On the first pass, read through the drivers and their assessment questions and write down the top drivers that you consider important. Write the list quickly, almost like a reflex response.

As you read the list, you may have noticed that most of the drivers are positive and attractive. They describe qualities many people want to have or wish they had. You may want to choose all 30 drivers. They all seem important. The truth is, not all 30 drivers really should get high marks from you. If you're really honest, not all 30 will be important to you. Most people are able to come up with around 10 on the first pass. Keep in mind that you're looking to uncover parts of yourself. Your drivers are an important foundation for your rewired lifestyle. It's worth it to hold up the mirror and see what's really *you*.

Quiz

Assessing Your Drivers

The drivers are listed in alphabetical order by the activity and then as evidenced in the person's life. They are not ranked by importance or popularity.

#1 Accomplishments—to have accomplishments

➡ Do you feel proud when you use your education, technical training, experience, or special skills in your work?

➡ Do you feel a sense of completion when you finish a work-related task or project?

➡ Do you like undertaking master assignments, expert tasks, or special projects?

#2 Action—to be "part of the action"

➡ Do you like work assignments that are high risk or give you an adrenaline rush?

➡ Do you enjoy being constantly on the go, living with tight deadlines?

➡ Do you like the buzz of a busy environment?

#3 Authority—to be an authority figure

➡ Do you like to be regarded as having all the answers?

➡ Do you enjoy having people seek you out for advice and counsel?

➡ Do you like to be perceived as an expert on a specific topic?

#4 Belonging—to have a sense of belonging

➡ Do you like to be part of a team, task force, management team, or special project team?

➡ Are you a member of a club, organization, or other group?

➡ Do you like to work for or be associated with a company or an organization?

#5 Competition—to be competitive

➡ Do you participate in activities where there is a recognized winner and loser?

➡ Do you like to win and get your way?

➡ Do you like the thrill of the game, the art of the deal?

#6 Creativity—to be creative

➡ Do you like to come up with novel ideas, to have your ideas challenged, or to think out of the box?

➡ Do you like to be part of brainstorming or idea-generating sessions?

➡ Do you look forward to being with people who see things differently from you?

#7 Current—to be current or "in"

➡ Do you like to "be up on the latest thinking," regardless of the topic?

➡ Do you like to be on the cutting edge or perceived as the one who always has the latest news?

➡ Do you like to be the first to see a new movie release, try a new restaurant, or buy a hot new item?

#8 Experiences—to have new experiences

➡ Do you seek out the opportunity for novel situations?

➡ Do you like meeting different, diverse people and having new experiences?

➡ Do you seek out different opinions?

#9 Friendship—to develop friendships

➡ Have you made most of your friends through work or work-related activities?

➡ Is your holiday greeting card list composed of people from work? From college? From social activities? Clubs? Memberships?

➡ Do you socialize with people from work in nonwork situations?

#10 Fulfillment—to be fulfilled

➡ Do you look for a sense of completion or satisfaction from what you do?

➡ Is it easy for you to identify what *doesn't* make you feel good about a job or task?

➡ Do you have a reason to jump up out of bed every morning? If not, do you want one?

#11 Global—to have global opportunities

➡ Do you seek out foreign assignments or go to foreign countries on vacation?

➡ Do you combine pleasure and business on overseas trips?

➡ Are you intrigued with globalization and multicultural issues?

#12 Goals—to have and to share goals

➡ Do you make New Year's resolutions and stick to them?

➡ Do you manage your time using a "to-do" list with defined objectives that you complete?

➡ Do you hate to feel goal-less?

#13 Identity—to have an identity

➡ Do you introduce yourself by saying what work you do?

➡ Does your work make you feel important?

➡ Do you need your business to identify who you are?

#14 Intellectual Stimulation—to be with intellectually stimulating people

➡ Will you accept a job because you want to work with a specific person?

➡ Does the best in you come out when others challenge your thinking?

➡ Do you feel better working with others who are smarter than you and/or do you like to be in mentally stimulating situations?

#15 Leadership—to be a leader

➡ Do you like to be the boss or the person responsible and have people follow you?

➡ Do you like the fact that you can motivate people to follow you and take up your mission?

➡ Do you often find yourself in charge and influencing others?

#16 Lifelong Learning—to be constantly learning

➡ Are you curious about and willing to entertain new concepts or unfamiliar processes?

➡ Do you have interests that you study just for the sake of knowledge?

➡ Do you research, take seminars on, attend lectures about, or read in-depth on topics that interest you outside your job requirements?

#17 Making a Difference—to help make the world better

➡ Do you like to do things that help others and make their lives better?

➡ Do you want to leave a legacy for your family, community, or society?

➡ Do you feel you have a bigger mission in life than the one you're presently fulfilling?

#18 Mentoring—to mentor others

➡ Are you known for taking people under your wing?

➡ Does it give you pleasure to help people grow?

➡ Do you take pride in helping others find or hone their skills and interests?

#19 Passion—to pursue a passion

➡ Is your work related to a personal passion, interest, hobby, or pastime?

➡ Would you do your job even if you didn't get paid to do it?

➡ Does your job fulfill you beyond the paycheck?

#20 People—to have exposure to people

➡ Do you find it stimulating to meet people at meetings, events, parties, and so on?

➡ Do you take an interest in the personal and family lives of team members, co-workers, people in the community, or associates?

➡ Do you hope to be close to people through work or personal activities?

#21 Power—to wield power

➡ Do you like to be in the position of deciding what happens?

➡ Do you like to be in charge and have the buck stop with you?

➡ Do you like to influence others at work or in social organizations?

#22 Prestige—to gain prestige

➡ Do you like people to look up to you or admire you?

➡ Do you like the halo effect you get from being associated with the "in" thing, company, or organization?

➡ Do you like to be associated with people who you feel enhance your image?

#23 Problem-Solving—to be a problem-solver

➡ Do you like to break down problems, solve them, and tie up all the loose ends?

➡ Do you like to get involved with jobs that others are having trouble completing?

➡ Do you like tackling tough tasks?

#24 Recognition—to be recognized

➡ Do you like people to acknowledge your importance by greeting you by name?

➡ Do you prefer to frequent restaurants where the staff knows you?

➡ Do you like it when the CEO or your co-workers publicly acknowledge your personal attributes, talent, or track record?

#25 Self-Esteem—to enhance self-esteem

➡ Do you look to work or co-workers to build your ego and give you confidence?

➡ Does positive feedback or kudos from others make you feel good?

➡ Do you look for situations or activities that make you feel good about yourself?

#26 Skills and Talent—to develop skills and talent

➡ Do you seek out opportunities where you can use your skills and talent?

➡ Do you embrace change and new ideas as the chance to test your skills and talent?

➡ Are you constantly trying to make yourself a better worker or person?

#27 Social—to be connected to others

➡ Are you happier being alone or with others?

➡ Do you need others to energize you?

➡ Are people and friends your lifeline to society?

#28 Structure—to have structure

➡ Do you prefer a highly developed organizational structure?

➡ Do you have a weekday and weekend work and/or personal routine?

➡ Do you get thrown when something doesn't go as planned or expected?

#29 Value—to give value to others or to be valued

➡ Do you like your clients, peers, boss, or associates to rely on you?

➡ Do you approach your work with the desire to become indispensable?

➡ Is it important to be valued by people you value? By anyone?

#30 Visibility—to have visibility

➡ Do you like to see your name mentioned in the paper or on a program, or hear it mentioned by others?

➡ Do you volunteer so you can strut your stuff?

➡ Do you sit at the front of the room at meetings, presentations, and religious services?

At this point, you should be completing your first pass. Which drivers did you select? You should have identified 5 to 10.

Identifying drivers is simple if you focus on drivers that are really you. Don't complicate the selection process with "shoulds" or "should-drivers," those you think you should have. 'Tis a gift to be simple, 'tis a gift to be free, as the Shaker song says. This is your time of freedom. Forget about what anyone else tells you, including spouses, friends, and children. No one should be looking over your shoulder on this journey of discovery.

Second Pass

The second pass is the time to reassess the list of drivers you made in the previous section. Chances are, you'll want to make some changes at this stage. Take a fresh look at the 5 to 10 drivers you identified. Reassess what you wrote on the list if it's been a few days. Do you still agree with what you selected, or do you want to make some changes? At this point, on your second pass through the list, you may be able to be more objective than you were when you first wrote it. Winnow your personal driver list to five drivers.

Reread the list of 30 drivers. Then reread your personal list of 5 to 10 drivers. As you do this, ask yourself these questions:

➡ Which drivers are key to me? Why?

➡ Which drivers make me feel the best?

➡ Which drivers have I consistently "owned" over my whole life?

➡ Which drivers aren't appropriate for me?

Think about these questions carefully. Which drivers have been with you the longest? Which drivers are newer? Look again at your personal list of 5 to 10 drivers. Which are the most important to you? Which ones aren't? Which ones can you eliminate from your list? Scratch off any driver that isn't "you." Do this until you have trimmed your personal driver list to just five drivers. These should be the drivers that are really important to you.

Third Pass

The third pass is the time when you take your list of five drivers and prioritize it. Take another break before you begin this pass. If you've done the previous two passes correctly, this time you should agree with yourself.

Do you have a list of five drivers that are important to you? Are you comfortable with the list? If so, you're ready now to rank your top five. Record your ranking. This is just one more step to help you identify what makes you tick.

Where Do You Stand?

At this point, you've completed all three passes, listing your five most important drivers in prioritized order. What makes you tick is right there in front of you, in black and white. What does that list tell you about your life? What does it say about who you really are?

Was the news good or bad? What does your list say about how much satisfaction you have in your life? How many of your drivers are fulfilled? Where are you finding fulfillment? Doing what? Which drivers are being fulfilled now? Which ones aren't? Are you satisfied or dissatisfied?

What can you do about it? What does your list require, ask, or demand of you? If you aren't getting driver fulfillment, what opportunity or direction could you seek to find fulfilling activities in the future? What opportunities does your list of drivers force you to consider? What will you need to do to find driver fulfillment? Have you been looking for driver fulfillment in the right places?

Did the list confirm your worst fears? Did you feel depressed when you saw it? Fearful? Did the list surprise you? Did you find yourself looking forward or back? Was it disconcerting? Puzzling?

Six Scenarios for Drivers

Based on our experience, people have a wide range of reactions to their list of drivers. On the one end, some people who are fulfilled at work look ahead to retirement with trepidation. Because they're fulfilled from work, how will they find fulfillment when work comes to an end? Does the end of work have to mean the end of driver fulfillment? On the other end of the spectrum, other people don't have and may never have had driver fulfillment at work. They look at their list of drivers and believe they either won't have drivers at all at retirement, they will fulfill their drivers in other ways, or they will have a new list of drivers.

In fact, we have found six different scenarios to describe how people react to their drivers. Which one describes you?

Driver fulfillment at work. If you have a pit in your stomach thinking about what will happen at retirement when you give up what fulfills your list of drivers, you are most likely in this category. You get a lot—sometimes even most—of your driver fulfillment at work. Your career or work is highly satisfying and motivates you to get out of bed in the morning. It fulfills parts of yourself that are deep inside you. If you're in this category, you're lucky in that you've been able to have driver fulfillment at work. Your question as you *rewire* is *How do I replace work I love?*

Driver fulfillment outside work. You leave your heart and soul at the door when you go to work. Work provides little driver fulfillment—sometimes none—but volunteer, unpaid, or other outside activities you are involved with do. You may be underestimating what you get from work such as routine, structure, and socializing with people. You may want to look at your job more closely. Your *rewire* question is *Why do these outside activities fulfill me more than my paid work?*

Driver fulfillment from previous work. With your list of drivers in front of you in black and white, it's very clear why you haven't been happy. The song line "You don't know what you've got 'til it's gone" was written for you. Your driver fulfillment came from a past job, position, career, or field. You'll need to give some more thought to why you liked what you used to do. Your *rewire* question is *How do I go back to what I used to like?*

Drivers not fulfilled. Some of you will look at your personal list of five drivers and realize that none of your drivers are fulfilled right now. Your work doesn't fulfill your drivers; it may never have. For you, retirement can be the opportunity of a lifetime, the chance to finally do something fulfilling because you have the time. You should think about your deferred dreams and special interests (see Chapter 6). Retirement can be the time for you to finally fulfill drivers doing things you were never able to do, for whatever reason.

But it can also be just another wasted opportunity. Some people never take the bull by the horns, even when they have the chance. Paying the mortgage keeps people from driver fulfillment, for one thing. Economics can be a serious impediment. But we also know of many people who said they could never afford to find fulfillment and they manage not to find it at retirement, either.

What happens to these people when retirement comes? Many just go with the flow. They don't seek opportunities, and they don't seek fulfillment either. Many feel that it's enough to just be with family or by themselves. For some, it will be. For others, it won't. Don't get us wrong. If you don't want to look for driver fulfillment, we're not knocking that choice; we're just asking the question. Which choice will you make? If you've come this far, you need to ask yourself the question, *How much do I want it?* Rewiring doesn't happen by itself. You have to go out and find it. After all, even being with yourself you can strive to fulfill some of your drivers. What will you do? Go with the flow or go for it? Which will it be? Your *rewire* question is *Will I seek driver fulfill-ment?*

Discard drivers. Many people look at their list of drivers and want to toss it out completely at retirement and wash their hands of the whole idea of drivers. "Drivers won't have anything to do with me at retirement," they say. Having worked a whole lifetime, people can't wait to get rid of anything that reminds them of work.

From our experience, it's hard to project into the future, but it's important to remember that these drivers have been with you a long time, and just because you want to relinquish them, it doesn't mean that 12 months from now you'll feel the same way. For one thing, you'll probably have a lot of time on your hands. As we said earlier, at age 65, you'll live on average another 22 years if you're a woman, another 18 if you're a man. We think it's best not to discard too much too soon. You may come back after some time has passed and realize your drivers mean more to you than you thought. Your *rewire* question is *What will drive me if my drivers don't?*

New drivers. Others look forward to retirement as the chance for a clean break. At retirement, they want a completely new stage of life. A new broom sweeps clean, as the saying goes. So these people want a new list of drivers to go along with their new lifestyles. Their new drivers represent a change from past work, communities, or lifestyles. For example, a college professor in New Jersey whose drivers were authority, lifelong learning, mentoring, and structure moved to Florida at retirement to live on the water and sail at least once a day. He rewired with new drivers—challenges, friendship, and passion. If you want to replace your old drivers with new ones when you *rewire*, this category fits you, and your *rewire* question is *What life will fulfill my new drivers?*

Where do you come out? Which of these six scenarios describes you best?

Real Quotes

There's a big difference between having a career and having a life. Be sure not to confuse the two.

—Barbara Bush, Wake Forest University Commencement Address (May 21, 2001)[2]

The Four Pre-Retirees

It's now time to return to the four pre-retirees you met in Chapter 1—Tom, Paula, Bob, and Carol—and see how they identified their drivers. When we first met them in Chapter 1, Tom, Paula, Bob, and Carol had already completed the first step in the *rewire* process. They made it clear that they viewed traditional retirement as a going *from* and rewiring as a going *to*. They also knew that traditional retirement wasn't for them, and they were more interested in rewiring as an alternative to traditional retirement.

They are now ready for step two in the *rewire* process—identifying their drivers. Brief thumbnail sketches of each of the four pre-retirees are given here, along with their drivers. A shortened version of the pre-retirees' stories is also given. (Refer to Chapter 1 if you want to read their whole stories.)

Now that you're familiar with drivers, as you read the pre-retirees' stories, you may want to see if you can pick out their drivers.

Real People: Tom

Tom, 58, is a national sales manager who develops winning sales teams year after year. He enjoys people and is the life of most parties. Tom is a goal-driven, well-organized manager who provides good structure and feedback to his people, but he hates the paperwork, meetings, and corporate reporting his job entails. He also misses being able to spend as much time on an individual basis with each of his salespeople, to coach them and bring them along.

A few months ago, the company turned down Tom's request for a "stepping down" initiative. He is looking at retirement in six months. Tom is in denial that he'll miss anything about his career. Golf is his passion. He thinks his two retirement goals—golf, golf, and more golf, and bringing his handicap down to 0—are all he needs.

Tom's drivers are as follows:

#5 Competition—to be competitive

#12 Goals—to have and to share goals

#18 Mentoring—to mentor others

#27 Social—to be connected to others

#28 Structure—to have structure

Our feedback: Tom was shocked to see that mentoring was one of his drivers. He hadn't realized that was such a strong component of his success at work, nor had he realized how much he hadn't been able to fulfill that driver at work because of his management duties. But he truly enjoys taking people under his wing and gets real pleasure in seeing them develop. Perhaps he can work mentoring into his retirement schedule some way. Tom has not faced the problem of what he'll do when the golf course is closed, especially in the winter months. Can he organize social events at the golf club? His wife doesn't play golf. How will he include her?

Real People: Paula

Paula is in her mid-60s. The first time she retired, she realized that work was her primary intellectual stimulation and outlet for her problem-solving skills. Well known in her industry, she got another job in human resources management. A few years later, she was tired and retired for the second time and discovered sailing. She loves sailing, spends all her spare time at it, and has quickly mastered it enough to be able to compete. Her daughter asked her to consult for the technology company where she worked. Paula created and implemented policies that solved staffing issues and was hired as the head of human resources. Paula eventually left her daughter's tech firm to start her own HR outsourcing/consulting firm, focusing on the needs of technology start-ups. Paula wants to keep both sailing and working in her life, but she isn't sure how to do it.

Paula's drivers are as follows:

#8 Experiences—to have new experiences

#14 Intellectual Stimulation—to be with intellectually stimulating people

#23 Problem-Solving—to be a problem-solver

#29 Value—to give value to others or to be valued

#30 Visibility—to have visibility

Our feedback: Paula wants to "balance." She wants to keep her hand in professionally but cut back on the hours and spend as much time as she can sailing. She says that having "retired completely" twice before with mixed results, she doesn't want to do that again. Paula is a quick study and realizes that she's her own HR problem. She needs to expand the options she'll consider and spend some time coming up with creative ideas. At this point, she's drawn a blank and isn't sure how to have her cake and eat it, too.

Real People: Bob

Bob is a 60-year-old senior engineer at an automotive company. In addition to his engineering responsibilities, he's in charge of the company outreach initiatives (both inside and outside the company). He is the go-to guy for complicated technical problems in engineering and keeps up with new applications and technologies. He is adept at bringing different groups of people together, and he loves the community-service aspect of his job because of the recognition he gets from the company. Bob is nervous about quitting work for good and wants to ask for a "phased" role for himself.

Bob's drivers are as follows:

#3 Authority—to be an authority figure

#4 Belonging—to have a sense of belonging

#16 Lifelong Learning—to be constantly learning

#17 Making a Difference—to help make the world better

#24 Recognition—to be recognized

Our feedback: Bob would like to "straddle" in retirement— to have one foot in the professional world and one foot in the community-service world and build a schedule that has some of the best of each. He has shared many of his questions. It's great, he admits, to be a volunteer when he's on someone else's pay-roll. But how will he feel about it when he's volunteering on his own nickel? Is community service something he really wants to continue to do? Is it an avocation or a vocation?

Real People: Carol

Carol, 51, just fell into Wall Street and never saw herself as a "financial person." But she has done very well financially, in spite of the fact that making other people rich was never personally fulfilling to her. She is beginning to think about what she'll do next.

What turns her on is being a catalyst for change. For years now, she has been an active supporter of politicians she believes will make a difference. A people person, she has an extensive business and social network she keeps in touch with and who are important to her. She loves dogs and keeps several English Setters as pets. When she recently became aware of how many animals are put down each year, she decided to make it her life's calling to save more animals.

Carol's drivers are as follows:

#2 Action—to be "part of the action"

#10 Fulfillment—to be fulfilled

#13 Identity—to have an identity

#17 Making a Difference—to help make the world better

#20 People—to have exposure to people

Our feedback: Carol doesn't have any doubts. She is ready to leave Wall Street behind. She is also comfortable with her drivers and wasn't surprised by any of them. She has lots of questions having to do with choices. *Do I want to do fund-raising? Do I want to build an organization? Do I want to work in a political appointment that affects animals in my state? Would a major dog food company hire me as an outreach coordinator to help raise funds to save dogs?*

Wrap-Up

Were you able to guess the pre-retirees' drivers? Did any surprise you? Can you see the diversity of their drivers? Knowing their stories, do you see how they find (or didn't find) driver satisfaction in their work? Bob is in the enviable position of satisfying his making a difference driver through additional responsibilities on company outreach initiatives. But how will he straddle that going forward? Paula finds the problem-solving and intellectual stimulation of her work in human resources fulfilling but isn't sure how to balance it with sailing.

The pre-retirees' stories also illustrate how some drivers aren't fulfilled at work. Carol has never found fulfillment from working on Wall Street and hopes that saving animals will provide driver fulfillment. Tom had forgotten how important mentoring was to him because he had gotten so bottom line–oriented, but he knows he wants golf, golf, and more golf. Is his desire for golf, golf, and more golf real or fantasy? Stay tuned.

Work can't fulfill all our drivers—human beings are too complex for that. But if you stay open to the expanded definition of work we propose throughout the book, we believe that as you *rewire*, you'll find fulfillment for your personal list of drivers you've selected.

Think about yourself for a moment. Now that you know what your drivers are, where in your life are you satisfying them? Where is your driver satisfaction coming from? What will happen when work is taken away? In Chapter 5, we'll answer those questions and more when we move to the exciting third step in the *rewire* process, linking the drivers to your activities. As you contemplate rewiring, you need to think about this: activities that provide you with driver fulfillment now will go away at retirement time. How will you replace them?

Earlier in the book, we said we would show you how to *know what you'll be leaving behind and then how to replace it when you rewire.* Coming to the end of this chapter, we acknowledge that for many of you, work may never have fulfilled your drivers. For you, we will show you how to *know what you have never gotten all these years and how to find it when you rewire.* Are you ready to find out?

Step III

Linking the Drivers to Your Activities

Chapter 5
What's Going to Go Away?

Retirement? The next Monday, I woke up and nobody is call-ing me, no clients are complaining, nobody's trying to sell me something—I'm sitting in the sun, disconnected from the world.

—*Stanley, 75, former advertising executive[1]*

Get ready to put your life under a microscope. This chapter is about the work-related activities that go away at retirement time. You already know your rewired energy is part of you and won't go away when you retire, but work-related activities *do* go away—and they leave a blank canvas.

Your activities create your opportunities for driver fulfillment. We call these driver-fulfilling activities *driver payoffs*. If you don't look in detail at your driver payoffs, you won't know which work-related activities to select to build a driver-fulfilling rewired life.

Driver fulfillment is highly individualized, and so are driver payoffs. To *rewire*, you need to know which activities are driver-fulfilling *for you*. The driver payoffs for your belonging driver, for example, are probably different from what your best friend does to fulfill that same driver. Remember, in the customized world of drivers and driver payoffs, one size doesn't fit all. In this chapter, you identify your driver payoffs and see exactly where your opportunities for driver fulfillment come from in your calendar. Doing this helps you know how to fill in the blank spaces in your calendar at retirement time.

The Three A's of Driver Payoffs

Although driver payoffs are highly individual, they share three common features, or the three A's of driver payoff, as we call them:

➡ Activity

➡ Audience

➡ Applause

When you identify your driver payoffs, you need to consider all three.

Activity

Activity is what you do to fulfill your drivers. Activities that fulfill drivers and driver payoffs are the same thing. In this chapter, you do a calendar analysis so you can see the links between your drivers and your activities. By the end of this chapter, you will have looked at every activity you have and know exactly what kind of opportunity it provides to fulfill your drivers.

Audience

Audience refers to the social side of driver payoffs, to the people you do your activities with. Drivers don't happen in a vacuum. The social side of driver payoffs is important because you probably won't like an activity if you don't like the people you're doing it with. Later in this chapter, you assess the audiences served by your activities as either very important, important, or less important. Think about these questions:

➡ Whom do I like doing things with?

➡ How important are these people to me?

➡ Are the people as important as the activity?

➡ Whom do I like to be with?

➡ Who are my friends?

➡ Do I like spending time with my peers/friends?

➡ What social groups do I feel comfortable with?

➡ What kinds of communities do I want to be involved with?

➡ As a volunteer, what kinds of people do I like to work with (either as workers or as clients)?

➡ Do I like to work with groups that share a common mission or purpose?

➡ Do I prefer to be in groups that are all men, all women, or mixed?

➡ Do I want to be involved with people in my same social, economic, or professional group?

➡ Do I want to be involved with people from different backgrounds?

➡ Do I like all my social networks to be the same or different?

Your answers to these questions will have great impact on your *rewirement* planning.

Tip

You want to make a difference … but to whom? Do you want to be involved in the hands-on dishing up of the soup? Or do you want to head up the fund drive that raises the money? Do you want to knock on the doors of restaurants, asking for the food? When you give, who do you want to receive?

Applause

What keeps you going? If you're like most people, you work for more than money; the pats on the back are important, too. The third A of driver payoffs, applause, includes the *attaboys/attagirls*, accolades, praise, positive feedback, and any other kind of recognition you enjoy getting from others. These types of recognition all boil down to the same thing—acknowledgment that makes you feel good. Applause makes a big difference as to whether you like your driver payoffs or not.

Applause is not the same as audience. *Audience* refers to the people you like to associate with. *Applause* refers to the feedback, the connection you get from people. We all like to be recognized, but the key thing is to know who you like to get your applause from.

Calendar Analysis

Are you ready to put your life under the microscope? At this point, you're going to pull out your calendar, put on your thinking cap, and examine your personal schedule in a way you never have before—in terms of driver payoffs.

Most people don't give much thought to whether their daily activities fulfill their drivers. Their calendars are just there, and they grow in response to other people, events, and outside pressures. And most people are too busy "doing life" to stand back, take a deep breath, and ask themselves what driver fulfillment they get from their daily activities.

Calendar analysis isn't time management. It isn't even about time, per se. To illustrate, we show you the results of the calendar analysis of two of the pre-retirees, Tom and Paula. Of the four pre-retirees, Tom and Paula are less sure of what they want to do when they *rewire* than Carol and Bob, so their thought processes are more interesting to follow. Because of their overlapping work and personal schedules, weekday and weekend calendars are given for both.

Real People: Tom

Tom, 58, is a national sales manager and has been in sales all his life. As a kid, Tom played sports. After games, his dad would always say to him, "Aim for the highest rung on the ladder. Raise your own bar. Compete against yourself." A career in sales allowed Tom to do all that, giving him monetary and personal fulfillment. As you'll see, Tom is in the fortunate position of getting a lot of driver fulfillment at work. But for the past few years, as corporate pressures have increased, Tom has struggled to maintain sales, let alone grow them, while at the same time manage layoffs and motivate the remaining staff. No matter what he and his staff did, it was never enough. Clients wanted deals. Management wanted profits. Tom wanted out.

As Tom began to look at his calendar, he grimaced when he saw the number of meetings he attended. He couldn't believe how much communication he was responsible for, the client dinners, the golf games (even though he was a golf fanatic), and the yearlong list of conferences and conventions he had to travel to attend. Now he knew why he was burned out!

Tom, who is planning to retire in six months, was both excited and hesitant about really looking at his calendar. He wasn't sure what he would really see once he opened up his eyes. Tom looked at a typical day to see what he really did. He knew he was busy, but at what?

Here are Tom's calendars.

Tom's Typical Weekday Calendar

5:30 A.M.	Rise
6:45	Work out at gym; watch CNBC
8:00	Breakfast meeting with friend's son who is thinking about going into sales
9:30	Weekly meeting with president and CFO regarding sales forecasts
11:00	Phone interview with editor of sales magazine on "How to Handle Difficult Clients Who Are Half Your Age"
Noon	Major client pitch and luncheon
2:45 P.M.	Interview new salesperson candidate
3:30	Market Research presents findings on customer service improvement
4:45	Talk to golf club director about upcoming corporate golf outing
5:00	Virtual biweekly sales meeting with national staff
7:30	Dinner with sales manager for more in-depth update
10:00	Say good night to wife and kids over cell phone on way home

continues

continued

Tom's Typical Weekend Calendar

Saturday:

8:00 A.M.	Five-mile run; record cumulative mileage toward annual goal
9:00	Read and comment on salespeople's weekly account activity
Noon	Lunch at golf club
1:00 P.M.	Tee off with a client and friends
5:00	Talk to golf pro about golf clinic Tom is organizing for clients
8:00	Flight to industry conference starting the next morning in Las Vegas
Sunday:	Industry conference in Las Vegas (through Tuesday)

Tom's Driver Payoffs

Next, Tom completes the third *rewire* step, linking his drivers to his activities, by going through his calendars and writing his drivers on his weekday and weekend calendars. Tom's drivers (identified in Chapter 4) are as follows:

#5 Competition—to be competitive

#12 Goals—to have and to share goals

#18 Mentoring—to mentor others

#27 Social—to be connected to others

#28 Structure—to have structure

Tom's Typical Weekday Calendar with His Drivers

5:30 A.M.	Rise (drivers: competition and structure)
6:45	Work out at gym; watch CNBC (drivers: competition and structure)
8:00	Breakfast meeting with friend's son who is thinking about going into sales (driver: mentoring)

9:30	Weekly meeting with president and CFO regarding sales forecasts (drivers: competition, goals, structure)
11:00	Phone interview with editor of sales magazine on "How to Handle Difficult Clients Who Are Half Your Age" (no driver fulfillment)
Noon	Major client pitch and luncheon (drivers: competition, goals, social, structure, and possibly mentoring if a new or young salesperson is present)
2:45 P.M.	Interview new salesperson candidate (no driver fulfillment)
3:30	Market Research presents findings on customer service improvement (no driver fulfillment)
4:45	Talk to golf club director about upcoming corporate golf outing (driver: social)
5:00	Virtual biweekly sales meeting with national staff (drivers: competition, goals, structure)
7:30	Dinner with sales manager for more in-depth update (drivers: goals, mentoring, social)
10:00	Say good night to wife and kids over cell phone on way home (driver: structure)

Tom's Typical Weekend Calendar with His Drivers

Saturday:

8:00 A.M.	Five-mile run; record annual mileage toward annual goal (drivers: competition, goals, structure)
9:00	Read and comment on salespeople's weekly account activity (drivers: goals, mentoring, structure)
Noon	Lunch at golf club (driver: social)
1:00 P.M.	Tee off with a client and friends (drivers: competition and social)
5:00	Talk to golf pro about golf clinic Tom is organizing for clients (drivers: competition and social)
8:00	Flight to industry conference starting the next morning in Las Vegas (no driver fulfillment)
Sunday:	Industry conference in Las Vegas (through Tuesday) (drivers: competition and social)

Tom's Personal Fulfillment Scorecard

Now for Tom's reality check: how frequently is he getting his driver payoffs? He'll find out when he creates a personal fulfillment scorecard. To do this, Tom counts how many times he has written a particular driver in his calendars. Tom sees, for example, that he has *competition* nine times, *structure* eight times, *social* seven times, *goals* seven times, and *mentoring* four times. Tom then lists the activities that fulfill these drivers (driver payoffs). He adds the things that give him no driver fulfillment. Tom's personal fulfillment scorecard, with drivers and driver payoffs from most to least frequent, follows.

Tom's Personal Fulfillment Scorecard

Drivers	Driver Payoffs
#1 Competition	getting up
	workouts and five-mile runs
	weekly meetings
	client pitch
	virtual biweekly sales meetings
	dinner with sales manager
	tee off with clients and friends
	talk to golf pro about golf clinic for clients
	industry conference
#2 Social	client pitch luncheon
	talk to director about the golf outing
	dinner with sales manager
	lunch at the golf club
	golf
	talk to pro about the golf clinic for clients
	industry conference
#3 Structure	getting up
	workouts and five-mile runs
	corporate meetings and dinners with sales staff
	client pitches

Drivers	Driver Payoffs
	reading and commenting on salespeople's weekly account activity on Saturday
	saying good night to family
#4 Goals	weekly corporate meetings
	client pitch
	talk to club director about golf outing
	dinner with sales manager
	lunch at the golf club
	golf
	golf clinic for clients
	industry conference
#5 Mentoring	breakfast with friend's son who is thinking about going into sales
	client pitch (if new or young salesperson is present)
	dinner with sales manager
	reading and commenting on salespeople's weekly activity
No driver fulfillment	phone interview
	interview new salesperson candidate
	meeting about market research findings
	flying

Up until this point, Tom knew what his drivers were, but they were more of an idea to him. He wasn't sure where his driver fulfillment came from. As he looks at his personal fulfillment scorecard, he sees how they come to life—*in his life.* For example, a major client pitch fulfills four of his drivers (competition, goals, social, and structure), with a fifth thrown in (mentoring) if a new or young salesperson is with him. Tom will use this as a guide to help him identify which driver payoffs will be important to him when he rewires.

Tom's Audiences

Lastly, Tom lists the audiences he serves with each activity on his calendars. What kinds of people does he relate to for each of his activities? He writes the generic categories of people he relates to and ranks each as very important, important, or less important, as follows:

Very important:

>   Family

>   Clients

>   President

>   Sales staff

Important:

>   CFO

>   Friend's son who wants to go into sales

>   Friend whose son wants to go into sales

>   Golf buddies

>   Pro at golf club

Less important:

>   People at the gym

>   Market research staff

>   Editor at sales magazine

>   Readers of the sales magazine he's interviewed by

>   Attendees at industry conferences

Some of the people Tom sees as very important will continue to be very important to him when he rewires, and some probably won't. For example, he loves mentoring. The people he mentors are important to him, people such as his friend's son who wants to go into sales. Will he want to find new outlets for his mentoring driver? He is surprised that casual colleagues and acquaintances are less important to him, but being part of an executive team is important.

Tom's Calendar—at Retirement

Next, Tom takes his calendar and takes out everything work-related *as though it's already retirement time.* What remains? A lot of blank space. What will he do? His gray cells get going, and he starts to jot down notes and questions to himself. For example, on his calendar he used to get up at 5:30 A.M. No way is he getting up at 5:30 anymore, he writes, but when will he get up? He jots more notes. As Tom does this, queries and ideas pop up. The rewired planning process has already begun. Tom's calendar—as though it's already retirement time—follows (weekday and weekend calendars are combined).

Tom's Combined Weekday and Weekend Calendar at Retirement—with Questions to Himself

5:30 A.M.	Rise—*no way am I getting up at 5:30 anymore! Getting up won't be about getting the competitive juices flowing anymore, but when will my day start?*
6:45	Work out at gym; watch CNBC—*look for a new gym because the company gym will no longer be available? Or will it? Ask about "retiree" membership privileges? Can the gym be more of a social thing now? What time do I want to go? Who else goes? Where and when?*
8:00	Breakfast meeting with friend's son who is thinking about going into sales—*I would still like to mentor. How can I help if I'm not connected to a corporation?*
	?
	?
Noon	Lunch at golf club—*whom will I have lunch with? When does the club close for the winter?*
1:00 P.M.	Tee off—*whom will I play golf with?*
	?
	?
4:45	Talk to golf club director about setting up golf outings—*is there a club outing coming up soon? Where does the pro go in the winter? Where do people play golf in the winter?*
	?
	?
10:00	Say good night to family—*definitely not from my cell phone in the car!*

Tom had complained about his schedule but was now shocked to see that he would have little to complain about in the future because most of his dislikes would remain behind when he walked out the door:

Leaving behind:

> Meetings, reporting, planning, account follow-up (day time and dinner time)
>
> Pitching business, being interviewed for articles
>
> Job interviews
>
> Industry conferences, client lunches, meetings
>
> Business travel

Keeping:

> Getting up in the morning
>
> Workouts and runs
>
> Golf
>
> Talking to the golf pro
>
> Mentoring his friend's son
>
> Saying good night to his family

It's easy to complain about something … until you don't have it to complain about anymore!

Real People: Paula

Now it's Paula's turn to look at her calendar. Paula is in her mid-60s and owns an HR outsourcing firm. She has retired twice already so she knows she's not good at ending things. She knows herself well—that's the good and the bad news. Having lived in foster homes until the age of 10, Paula never really had a family of her own, and she gets attached to her workplace and her clients. She tends to view them as extended family, including them in her overlapping social and business activities. For Paula, business and personal are cloth cut from the same piece. She needs to be visible and to have a positive impact in communities that she values and where she is valued.

Here are Paula's calendars.

Paula's Typical Weekday Calendar

7:45 A.M.	Sit on panel at industry business/networking breakfast seminar
10:00	Meet potential new client to assess needs
Noon	In office: review e-mails and voicemails; lunch at desk
1:00 P.M.	Marketing meeting to discuss direct mail marketing brochure
2:00	Meeting with business associate on final draft of report on "Using Independent Knowledge Workers Effectively"
4:00	Participate in conference call as member of nonprofit board's executive search committee
4:45	Meet with accountant about office space lease and payment issues
5:00	Staff meeting giving an update on business development
6:00	Drinks with potential client
8:00	Honoree at black-tie industry reception

Paula's Typical Weekend Calendar

Saturday:

9:00 A.M.	Outline or complete writing articles for industry publication while sitting on the deck at home
Noon	Conduct sailing course for young girls
2:00 P.M.	Errands and shopping
6:00	Local hospital fund-raising dinner

Sunday:

9:30 A.M.	Reading business journals and mail
Noon	Sailing with daughter

Paula's Driver Payoffs

Next, Paula writes down the drivers fulfilled by each activity in her calendars. Paula's drivers are:

#8 Experiences—to have new experiences

#14 Intellectual Stimulation—to be with intellectually stimulating people

#23 Problem-Solving—to be a problem-solver

#29 Value—to give value to others or to be valued

#30 Visibility—to have visibility

Paula's Typical Weekday Calendar with Her Drivers

7:45 A.M.	Sit on panel at industry business/networking breakfast seminar (drivers: intellectual stimulation, value, visibility)
10:00	Meet potential new client to assess needs (drivers: intellectual stimulation, problem-solving, value)
Noon	In office: review e-mails and voicemails; lunch at desk (no driver fulfillment)
1:00 P.M.	Marketing meeting to discuss direct mail marketing brochure (driver: problem-solving)
2:00	Meeting with business associate on final draft of report on "Using Independent Knowledge Workers Effectively" (drivers: problem-solving, value)
4:00	Participate in conference call as member of nonprofit board's executive search committee (drivers: intellectual stimulation, problem-solving, value)
4:45	Meet with accountant about office space lease and payment issues (driver: problem-solving)
5:00	Staff meeting giving an update on business development (drivers: intellectual stimulation, problem-solving)
6:00	Drinks with potential client (drivers: problem-solving, value)
8:00	Honoree at black-tie industry reception (driver: visibility)

Paula's Typical Weekend Calendar with Her Drivers

Saturday:

9:00 A.M.	Outline or complete writing articles for industry publication while sitting the deck at home (drivers: intellectual stimulation, visibility)
Noon	Conduct sailing course for young girls (drivers: experiences, problem-solving, value)
2:00 P.M.	Errands and shopping (no driver fulfillment)
6:00	Local hospital fund-raising dinner (drivers: value, visibility)

Sunday:

9:30 A.M.	Reading business journals and mail (no driver fulfillment)
Noon	Sailing with daughter (drivers: experiences, problem-solving)

Paula's Personal Fulfillment Scorecard

Now it's time for Paula to create her personal fulfillment scorecard. She counts how many times she wrote down each driver on her calendars. In order of frequency, Paula's drivers are *problem-solving* (nine), *value* (six), *intellectual stimulation* (five), *visibility* (four), and *experiences* (twice). Three activities provide no driver fulfillment. Paula's personal fulfillment scorecard, with drivers and driver payoffs from most to least frequent, follows.

Paula's Personal Fulfillment Scorecard

Drivers	Driver Payoffs
#1 Problem-Solving	meetings and drinks with clients and potential clients
	meet to discuss direct mail marketing brochure
	meet with associates to review final draft reports
	conference call as member of nonprofit board
	meet with accountant about office space issues

continues

Paula's Personal Fulfillment Scorecard   *continued*

Drivers	Driver Payoffs
	staff meeting giving update on business development
	conduct sailing course for young girls
	sail with daughter
#2 Value	sit on panel at industry business/networking seminar
	meetings and drinks with clients and potential clients
	meet with business associates on final drafts of reports
	participate as member of nonprofit board
	conduct sailing course for young girls
	local hospital fund-raising dinner
#3 Intellectual Stimulation	sit on panel at industry business/networking seminar
	meetings and drinks with clients and potential clients
	participate as member of nonprofit board
	staff meeting giving an update on business development
	write articles for industry publications
#4 Visibility	sit on panel at industry business/networking seminar
	honoree at black-tie reception
	write articles for industry publications
	local hospital fund-raising dinner
#5 Experiences	sail with daughter
No driver fulfillment	conduct sailing course for young girls
	reviewing office e-mails and voicemails
	errands and shopping
	reading business journals and relaxing

Paula is beginning to itch for change. She has hung on to her business because many of her activities involve people who have come to be like family to her and are part of her life, and she may have encouraged them not to be as independent as they could be. But does she really have to be involved in so many meetings? She is starting to tire of the administrative side and management hassles. She wonders if some other activities besides her business will fulfill her drivers. Paula has a *straddler* mentality. Her body is still in the present, but her mind is inching forward. Having retired completely twice before, she knows she has to figure out what she really wants so she doesn't repeat the same mistakes. If she figures that out, she tells herself, maybe it won't be as bad as she expects. She reasons that the key is to figure out how to take today's driver payoffs and convert them into new roles or activities that will fulfill her drivers in the future. But how?

Paula's Audiences

Paula now notes which audiences she feels are very important, important, or less important:

Very important:

> Daughter

> Clients

> Nonprofit board

> Young girls taking the sailing course

> Sailing partners

Important:

> Business associate working on the draft report

> Industry clients and potential clients

> Community (hospital board)

Less important:

> Industry colleagues

> Marketing staff she reviews the brochure with

> Readers of the industry publication she writes for

Paula wants to keep her very important audiences as she rewires. She realizes that her clients are more important to her than her business associates. She also realizes that the audiences from her visibility-driver-payoff activities (for example, industry conferences, potential clients, and readers of the industry publication she writes for) are less important to her than either of the other two. Perhaps the visibility driver isn't that important anymore. Is there something else that's more important now? Perhaps she won't miss it if she cuts back on the conferences, seeking new clients, and writing articles, she muses. And she is itching to sail more.

Paula's Calendar—at Retirement

Now Paula is ready to remove the work-related stuff from her calendar. Paula drops everything relating to her business, including clients, management of the office and the day-to-day business issues, the business conferences, and so on. Here's what she comes up with:

Leaving behind:

> Client contact—meetings, drinks, lunches
>
> Business management issues
>
> Writing articles
>
> Industry conferences, receptions, meetings

Keeping:

> Board work
>
> Sailing
>
> Conducting the young girls' sailing course

Paula gulps anxiously as she feels the impact of dropping clients from her list. She loves her clients. She then writes her calendar as though it's retirement time.

Paula's Combined Weekday and Weekend Calendar at Retirement—with Questions to Herself

6:15 A.M.	Rise
	?
9:30	?
	?
	?
Noon	Conduct sailing course for young girls—*weekend only. Is there a way to offer the course after school on weekdays?*
2:00 P.M.	Errands and shopping/sail with daughter—*weekend only*
4:00	Participate in conference call as a member of non-profit board's executive search committee
	?
6:00	Local hospital fund-raising dinner
	?
	?

Looking at her retirement calendar, Paula wonders if there's a way to get in more sailing on weekdays. What new roles can she find to fulfill her intellectual stimulation, problem-solving, and value drivers? And her clients still rank as very important. Is it crazy, she asks, or can she find a way to mix sailing and her clients?

Personal Calendar Analysis

Now that Tom and Paula have shown you how to do calendar analysis, it's time for you to do your own. You will do this in two steps:

1. Fill in your weekday and weekend calendar.
2. Add your drivers.

First, pick a typical day and write down everything you do that day by creating "Your Typical Weekday Calendar" and "Your

Typical Weekend Calendar." The day should be representative, containing a good selection of the activities you do on a typical day. Don't pick a day you're off from work or at an off-site conference. If your schedule varies widely from day to day, you can also create a composite day, one in which you include all your usual activities as though they happened on one day.

Next, add your drivers to each activity you wrote on "Your Weekday Calendar" and "Your Weekend Calendar." Refer to Chapter 4 for your drivers if you need to.

Your Personal Fulfillment Scorecard

Next, fill out your personal fulfillment scorecard. To do this, total up how many times you wrote down a particular driver on your calendar. For example, you may have written down the achievement driver a total of five times and the belonging driver twice. Write down each driver and its accompanying driver payoff (i.e., activity). Don't be shocked if you have only a few drivers fulfilled by your activities. What strikes you about your list? Where is your driver fulfillment coming from? Are you getting enough driver fulfillment? Looking ahead, how will things change at retirement time? Make a note of any reaction you have.

Your Audiences

Don't forget to identify your audiences. Ken, a rewiree we know, quit working at 60 but wanted to keep up his presence in the industry and continue to be known as an authority and expert after he was out of corporate America. When he left the company, Ken rolled into the presidency of an industry organization. Professional recognition from Ken's peers was very important to him. He chose a retirement career in which he would continue to be known among his colleagues for his expertise, but in a new setting. Make a note of which audiences are important to you and which aren't.

Your Calendar—at Retirement

Now, write on a blank sheet of paper your calendar without work-related activities, *as though it's retirement time.* Write your calendar (with weekday and weekend combined) with your work-related activities removed. The key questions are as follows:

➡ What's left?

➡ What fell away?

➡ How do you feel about that?

In our experience, pre-retirees are both positively and negatively surprised when they see what happens to their calendars. We're not out to jar you, but to show you how to have a seamless transition into rewiring. And to do that, you have to know what you own in your life, what you'll lose, what you'll want to replace.

The best *rewirements* are based on honesty with yourself and the recognition of what it really takes to fulfill your drivers. Take time to reflect. Which activities would you like to have again in the future? How might you find them? Which activities would you like to discard? Jot down any notes that come to mind.

Six Scenarios

How did you feel when you saw your blank calendar *as though it were retirement time?* Did it give you any surprising feedback about your job or your life? Did it bring to the surface the reasons why you want to stay at or leave your job? Did it bring you up short by showing you how much of your life either is or isn't fulfilling your drivers? We have seen six possible scenarios in response to the calendar exercise. Which one fits you? There are people who want to …

Keep working at current job. You've got a good thing going in your job and are staying in your current position, at least for now. You are getting enough driver fulfillment from what you do. Why stop now? This scenario occurs more frequently with entrepreneurs than corporate employees.

Slow down. You decide to stay in the same job or career but pursue a phased situation, or transition into part-time, seasonal, shared, or some other type of flexible paid work.

Get another job. You decide to get another job, often another full-time job. You feel you don't have enough other interests, hobbies, family, or other commitments that provide driver fulfillment. Work may have become a comfort zone.

Start the next act. You look forward to rewiring and are actively planning ahead. You're eager to move on and have lots of things lined up in a rewired life that will fulfill your drivers.

Get ready, but don't know what to do. You like your work and get driver fulfillment from it, and are ready to move on, but you're not sure what's ahead and wonder if you'll find enough other interests to fulfill you. You're probably ready but don't know it and will benefit from planning.

Get out. You get little driver fulfillment from your job and can't wait to get out. You've either got it all together or you're in deep denial.

What Else Goes Away?

Our research with retirees turned up other things they missed, things we haven't been able to cover so far in this chapter. Which of these will you miss when you *rewire?* Which will you want to try to keep?

Chit chat. You talk with people when you work. Colleagues, teammates, bosses, subordinates, clients, customers, even the security guards provide you with the chance to engage in chit chat, the informal banter that makes working fun.

Coffee klatch. Coffee klatch is the easy socializing you do with colleagues, customers, and friends at work. Work provides opportunities for refreshments and meals, along with the sharing that comes with the package. Many people report that they miss this kind of easy back and forth with co-workers. Do you enjoy this kind of socializing (birthdays, work celebrations, holiday lunches, etc.) with co-workers? If so, how will you replace it?

Office energy. Some offices have a buzz; others have hustle-bustle; others have noise. But no matter what you call it, all offices put out energy. It may be a co-worker's great laugh or your colleague's wisecracks that you will miss. Or it may be the general din of people getting things done. What will replace that?

Something bigger. Some people miss being involved with something larger than themselves. Maybe you miss being part of a team. If you like being part of something larger than yourself, where will you find a replacement for it?

Ritual. Work is more than just the office. You have to get there and back. Believe it or not, people miss the rituals associated with commuting—Starbucks, listening to the radio, stopping for a snack or the paper. Think about the things you do as you travel back and forth from work. They may have become an important part of the fabric of your life and may be something you'll miss. (Missing rituals may also mean the structure driver is important to you.) Where will you find replacement rituals after you stop working?

Feeling important. Work makes people feel important. By that, we don't mean just getting the *attaboys* and *attagirls,* discussed earlier in this chapter. For many people, work not only gives them something to do, it also makes them feel they have a role to fulfill and that feeling itself resonates on a deep level. Without this feeling of importance, people feel vulnerable. Think about your empty calendar. When you *rewire,* what will you have to make you feel important?

Who will make your phone ring? A friend of ours told us about his *rewire* transition. He went from a corporate career at a company where he had been for many years to running his own part-time consulting business. What he wanted when he rewired wasn't so much a professional identity (although that was important), but connections. "I don't know what I would have done if the phone didn't ring," he said. "I couldn't have faced that." Without having someone else to keep in touch with, it's easy to get too isolated. Whom do you want to call you? Whom do you want to make your phone ring? How will you stay connected?

Getting rewired is about taking a holistic approach to your planning. Now that you know what's going to fall away from your work calendar, the next chapter asks, "What are you doing with your free time?"

Chapter 6
What Are You Doing with Your Free Time?

Transition *is a better word than* retirement. *You need to plan ahead so you can make the transition to something that is new and creative.*

—*Jack, 84, former business professor*[1]

In the last chapter, we froze the frame when we showed you your calendar *as though it were retirement time.* Looking ahead to that freeze frame, it should have been pretty clear to you what's going to go away when you stop working. For most of you, the first place to start is to ask yourself if what you're doing right now fulfills your drivers. For many people, the things that will fulfill them in *rewirement* are already a part of their lives, but other people will have to develop new interests and activities to live a full life.

When work falls away, your free time will open up, leaving a lot of blanks. What will you have in your life when this happens? Will you be left with activities that fulfill you or just fill the time? Have you developed enough of a life outside work to fill in the blanks in ways you'll find fulfilling when you *rewire?* Do you have work/leisure balance? Or is work your life? This chapter poses the question: *Are you using your free time now doing or developing driver-fulfilling activities outside work?*

Blending Work and Leisure

One of the first things people realize when they get within a few years of retirement time is how much of their leisure is blended with work. Business entertaining meets social and personal needs for leisure, fun, and recreation for many people, as do company picnics and other company functions. Paula, one of our four pre-retirees, loves to sail and entertains her clients by sailing, often inviting her daughter to join them. Bob, the engineer, does many social activities as part of his community initiatives with the company, activities his wife also enjoys. And Tom, who loves golf, takes clients golfing and even organizes company golf outings.

Real Quotes

[A] growing number of highly successful knowledge workers of both sexes—business managers, university teachers, museum directors, doctors—"plateau" in their 40s. They know they have achieved all they will achieve. If their work is all they have, they are in trouble. Knowledge workers therefore need to develop, preferably while they are still young, a noncompetitive life and community of their own, and some serious outside interest—be it working as a volunteer in the community, playing in a local orchestra, or taking an active part in a small town's local government. This outside interest will give them the opportunity for personal contribution and achievement.

—Peter Drucker[2]

In Chapter 5, Tom and Paula began thinking about the adjustments they'll have to make when they're no longer working. They both spend a lot of their free time in blended business/pleasure activities. Paula isn't sure how she'll replace clients (who are like family to her) and the activities they did together in her rewired life. And Tom's company pays for his gym membership and underwrites many of his golf outings, including the golf club membership. Can he afford to pay for it? Will clients still want to play golf with him? Will their personal relationship transcend their business relationship?

How much do your business and pleasure activities overlap? How much of your travel is company-sponsored? Make a note of the activities that blend both. You'll have to find ways to replace business-sponsored leisure on your own when you *rewire*.

How Are You Using Your Free Time?

When you quit working, every day will become a vacation day. For some people, this is great; for others, it isn't. People ask, *What am I going to do with my free time when I* rewire? To answer this, let's see what you already have in terms of free time and also analyze your leisure activities. You first need to see exactly how you're spending your time now. We'll do this with a calendar analysis.

We used a calendar analysis in the previous chapter to link your drivers with your daily activities. Here, we take a longer, two-week time frame to take a more holistic view of your life and not leave anything out. Doing a two-week analysis includes things that don't come up as often in your schedule and that might become the basis of an activity you'd like to expand in your rewired life. To keep the focus on you, the reader, we've not analyzed the interests of the four pre-retirees in detail.

Analyzing your time also shows you how to get the most out of it, so you can use whatever free time (however scarce) you have to develop interests to expand on when you *rewire*. The time to start using your free time wisely is *now*. Even though you have a scarcity of free time in your working years and a surplus of it upon retirement, it's much easier to take at least one activity that's already in your life and expand upon it at retirement time than it is to start something that's brand new at retirement time. It's best to start to develop a life outside work when you're still working.

The first step to getting more out of the free time you have is to know how you are spending your free time now. Our goal is not to analyze your calendar, but to get you thinking about how much fun you're having with your free time. Take a look at your time over the past two weeks, and see what you did for fun with your free time. The following suggested free time diary categories might help you analyze your free time.

Art and culture
Dining (at home or out)
Education
Entertainment (arts, theater, movies)
Family
Friends, socializing
Games (cards, puzzles)
Health, exercise, therapy
Hobbies/interests
Internet
Investment management
Museums
Naps
Reading
Religion (services, holidays)
Shopping
Spiritual
Sports (fishing, tennis)
Television
Travel
Volunteering (community, civic)

Write down anything you're doing with your free time now that you find fulfilling. Then think about whether any of these fulfill your drivers. Ask yourself whether any of these activities will be impacted when you quit working. For example, Tom, one of our four pre-retirees, discovered that two weekends in a row he golfed with clients—something that might change when he quits working. Paula sailed with clients. And Bob took one of his co-workers to a World War I meeting. The more you really know about your life now, the better a rewired life you'll have and the easier the transition from work to *rewirement* will be.

In our experience, people have one of five reactions to their calendar analysis:

No leisure. Some people have focused so much on work that they haven't developed any outside activities. If you're in this position and you want to avoid boredom when you *rewire,* you need to develop the nonwork side of your life now.

Work and leisure are integrated. People whose work and leisure are blended have some issues to think through. Will they miss the company-sponsored leisure, and how will they replace it? What will they be able to afford? Will they take their friends with them, or will their friends stay behind?

Interests can be expanded. Some people have a lot of activities that can be expanded. For example, Paula, one of our pre-retirees, may be able to offer her sailing course for young girls more often.

Blank spaces are exciting. Some people find the unknown exciting. They look forward to filling in the blanks and aren't sure yet with what. They may have activities and interests they've deferred and will pursue when they have the time.

Activities can be discarded. Sometimes people look at their calendar, see lots of activities they don't like anymore, and say to themselves, *It's time to move on, now that I see my life in black and white.* They have lots of activities on their calendar that aren't great for them anymore and that they will discard.

The best-prepared rewired lives are those in which people build into their lives those activities they think they'll enjoy in *rewirement—while they are still working full-time.* We know time constraints make this difficult, but it's always possible to take small steps and start with a telephone call, a meeting, or an inquiry. Instead of waiting, start working on your rewired life now.

Driver-Fulfilling Free Time

A friend of ours whose drivers are to be current, part of the action, social, and to have exposure to people, paced back and forth on her two-week vacation at a secluded resort in St. Bart's. She wasn't ready to chill, and none of the enticements at the resort fulfilled her drivers. She was bored and—because she was bored—she had trouble relaxing.

If you've ever been on a vacation that was a disaster, we're willing to bet the problem was a mismatch between your drivers and your leisure activity. When you have a lot of free time and are doing activities that don't suit your drivers, you're going to be bored, or worse. And due to the surplus of free time upon retirement, every day is a vacation day. How will you find fulfillment then?

To answer this question, we focus on your drivers. We believe that driver-fulfilling free time leads to the greatest satisfaction. When you plan your leisure, you need to take your drivers into account. Of course, it's important to have a balance between driver-fulfilling activities and non-driver-fulfilling activities. Obviously, every activity in your life can't fulfill a driver. But our research showed the overriding importance of driver fulfillment in retirement satisfaction. And driver fulfillment doesn't just happen in work. It happens in leisure, too.

How do drivers come into the discussion of leisure? Let's say the competitive driver is important to you and you decide to fulfill it through sports. Your leisure sport should then have a competitive edge, such as competitive leagues, golf tournaments, contests, and so on. If you are a swimmer, for example, you won't be happy swimming laps in the pool by yourself, no matter how good the exercise is, because none of your friends are there to compete against—you're all by yourself. If you are on a team in a senior swimmer's meet, though, things will be better. Tom, the pre-retiree who is a salesperson, has the competitive driver and fulfills it in his leisure by recording the mileage of his daily runs and comparing it against that of his friends. He will probably continue to do that after he quits working. But will tracking his daily runs be enough to fulfill his competitive driver when he rewires?

Tip

Just because it's leisure doesn't make it fulfilling. Think about your drivers when you consider the most fulfilling activities from among the myriad leisure choices available.

Whose Driver Is It, Anyway?

Whose drivers are being fulfilled in your free time? Yours? Or someone else's? Are you going to the Yankees games because your spouse loves the Yankees or because you both do? His leisure isn't necessarily yours, and vice versa. Don't expect your idea of driver-fulfilling leisure to be anyone else's. Leisure and free time belong to both people in a couple and also to each person individually. Be sure everyone gets his or her turn.

Leisure Needs Change

Your leisure needs change after you quit working, and you need to factor this into the *rewirement* equation. Leisure activities that suited you when you were working full-time might not fulfill you after you quit.

For example, maybe you loved going to the theater after a hectic week at work, but sitting in the theater is an extremely passive experience. When you quit working, will you still find the theater engaging enough, or will you need to add something else more fulfilling? Maybe you'll want to go from being in the audience to being actively involved behind the scenes, staging the production, creating sets, making costumes, and so on. You might go from watching Broadway shows to putting on community theater shows. Again, to help you decide, keep your drivers in mind.

Plan Your Free Time

Start to plan now, even if you're working. We recommend starting at least five years before you plan to quit working full-time.

Use your work connections. It's easier to make connections while you're still working. Like it or not, your employer provides you with ready connections you can leverage and use to springboard into opportunities for rewired leisure activities. The unfortunate truth is that professional and business associations and even sports clubs may not want you when you're no longer with the company, but they'll often keep you on after you quit if they already know you. Take advantage of well-established business and professional connections while you're still employed. Join any clubs, social groups, or associations ahead of time.

Tip

Identify what activities and associations will end with retirement. Some things that end will be out of your control; others won't be. Recognize what endings you can control.

Things take time. If you apply for a position or for membership, it can take several months, even up to a year, or years, for you to be considered. Club memberships, social groups, sports leagues, and community and volunteer positions all take time.

One man we worked with wanted to become a docent at his favorite museum when he rewired. He loved everything related to Ancient Greece and had been a Classics major as an undergraduate. Being a docent was going to be pure pleasure for him. Unfortunately, he waited until December 31, after his retirement party, to look into it. He then learned that the museum required that he take a nine-month docent training course, which had already started the previous September, and that he would have to wait until the following September to take it. He hadn't done his homework, so he didn't know that he could have taken the once-a-week docent training classes while he was still working. He was going to end up wasting almost a whole year!

And what about the woman we know who wanted to read for the blind, but found out she was #399 on the volunteer list?

You might not be accepted into your leisure activity of choice. If you want to join a group playing tennis or a book group, for example, you often have to get to know people first, as many of these groups are by invitation only. Start investigating early, so you won't be left out.

What can you start doing now? An executive we know had the leisure goal of piloting his home-built airplane when he rewired. Because he was going to build the airplane himself, he knew he would have to start several years ahead so the airplane would be airworthy when he planned to quit working. He started building it nights and weekends when he was still working, first in the basement of his house and then in a local airport hangar. As his interest deepened, he became a member of the airport association and made friends with the other pilots. After several years, he exceeded his goal, piloting the plane successfully before he quit working, and had a circle of new friends and acquaintances.

Now that we've exposed the opportunities for leisure and fun, the next question is *What have you been holding inside?* In the next chapter, get ready to unearth dreams, passions, and interests that have been on hold.

Step IV

Creating Your Rewired Vision

Chapter 7
Dreams, Interests, and Discoveries

I'm going to clown school to become a clown. That's love, not work.

—Al, 60, former executive

Now that you've linked your drivers to what you *do*, it's time to focus on what you *dream of doing and being*. This chapter begins step four of the *rewire* process. When you *rewire*, you have the chance to become the person you were meant to be, if you aren't already, and to do the things you've always dreamed of doing. Rewiring is your time to focus on your discarded dreams, uninvestigated interests, delayed discoveries, and any of the stuff you haven't done or pursued because you were too busy "doing life."

In this chapter, you have a chance to let out your kite and let your imagination run wild. This is about *you*, so you shouldn't let anyone else look over your shoulder. This is your time to throw off all your personas and say "no" to all the voices chanting *shoulda, woulda, coulda*. Finding what is going to give you fulfillment in your rewired life involves investigating yourself in a number of different ways. This chapter is where you use your imagination. Finding your dreams, interests, and discoveries is about leaving the practical world behind and powering up your imagination. We believe that if you imagine it, it can happen. And we'll prove it can be done by showing you other people who've done it.

Rewiring might be the last chance you have to go for your dreams and interests and to make discoveries.

Life Is Fragile

September 11, 2001, had an unexpected impact on us, as authors of this book. Shortly after the attack, we received calls from the pre-retirees and retirees we had talked to months before, during our research for the book. When they called, they explained that the September 11 attack had made them rethink their priorities. They didn't want to wait any longer to achieve their dreams.

Molly is a corporate lawyer who had been a hippie during the Vietnam years and a political science major. Her dream has been to be an activist in her next life, or to run for public office. When she called, she explained that she was eager to get started on her dream now. She no longer wanted to wait until she retired to work activism into her life. She was investigating getting into local politics now.

And retirees called saying that it seemed even more important for them to be involved in volunteerism, whether on a large or small scale.

These are examples of a trend we have noticed. People are looking for their dreams *now*. We live a few miles from Ground Zero in Manhattan. The attacks reminded us that life is fragile. We expect to pass this way but once, as the saying goes, and if there's anything we can do, we shouldn't defer or neglect it, for we shall not pass this way again. Don't expect endless tomorrows. The time to follow your dreams is *now*.

What Are Your Dreams?

A dream is a wish or a fantasy with your thumbprint on it. It's something dear and special to you. If you ask most people what they've always dreamed of, they can usually tell you. Dreams are often right there on the surface, waiting for a prompt. For example, Phyllis is a stockbroker who knows exactly what she wants to do. She loves the Gilded Age and everything about it. Her dream is to walk in the footsteps of Edith Wharton and Henry James, both in the United States and in Europe. She wants to travel to the places where they lived and immerse herself in the lifestyle of the period.

Others might think your dreams are idiosyncratic, even weird. Don't listen to them! Gertie always dreamed of skydiving, and she finally did it. At age 79 she says, "I don't want my great-grandchildren to jump out of airplanes. It's dangerous; they can get killed. If they're 20, that would be a waste of 65 years. But if you've lived to 75 or 80, you've done and seen everything—so why doesn't everyone skydive at 80?"[1]

Dreams have the potential to become rewired careers if you start to plan early enough. Dave, 46, an insurance salesman, has always loved horses. He not only rides them but believes they are the most wonderful creatures on Earth. His sister, who had polio as a child, once rode a pony at a fair and said she "didn't feel broke anymore when she rode the pony." Dave's dream is to have a ranch/farm/facility (whatever he can afford) that offers physical therapy on horses for disabled children.

What are your dreams? What have you dreamed of but haven't done? Too many people are living someone else's dream. To figure out what your dreams are, complete the following three dream-catching exercises. We believe there's no single path to finding your dreams, so we offer different types of exercises with three different approaches. Try them all and see which one works best for you.

Dream-Catching Exercise #1

Ann Richards, the former governor of Texas, used an exercise similar to this when she figured out what she wanted to do after she left politics. She shared with us how the exercise works in a private interview. This exercise is especially poignant because Richards passed away in September 2006.[2]

For exercise #1, imagine you have five years to live. Write down everything you've ever dreamed about doing. Don't spend a lot of time thinking about this. Write down the first ideas that come to mind.

Now imagine you have one year to live. Write down everything you would want to do. Again, work quickly.

Lastly, imagine you have only three months to live. Write down everything you dream of doing.

Look at your answers for five years, one year, and three months. Circle the similar answers for all three. Which answers did you write all three times? Which did you write least? The things you wrote down more than once provide clues as to what your dreams are. Make a note of what you wrote; you come back to your answers later.

Dream-Catching Exercise #2

If you've completed exercise #1, you're ready to continue. Answer the following questions:

➡ Think back to your childhood. What excited you?

➡ What did you want to be when you were 5, 10, or 15 years old?

➡ When you hate your job, what do you wish you could do?

➡ What did you envy other people doing?

➡ What are your "someday" activities?

➡ When you can do whatever you want, what do you do?

➡ If money were no object, what would you want to do?

➡ What do you do with your personal time while on vacation?

Did any themes pop out? Do any similarities exist in what you wrote in exercises #1 and #2? Write down any answers that were the same.

Tip
People mourn that they don't have a passion, but not everyone is fortunate enough to have discovered one. Remember how important a balanced portfolio is for your investments? Why not strive to have a balanced portfolio of dreams, interests, and discoveries that fulfill your drivers? Don't postpone your life looking for that one ultimate passion!

Dream-Catching Exercise #3

Look over your answers in exercises #1 and #2, and note the recurring themes. The following are common phrases people use to introduce their dreams. What have you heard yourself say when you've used one of these phrases? How will you answer these phrases?

➡ It's never too late to …
➡ One day I'll …
➡ One of these days I'll …
➡ If I had the money, I'd …
➡ If I had the time, I'd …
➡ You never know, I just might …
➡ If only I could …

Your someday is now. You're ready to declare your dream. What have you decided to no longer delay?

The Sky's the Limit

One rewiree we interviewed was always interested in radio. He had ham radios, always listened to *The Shadow* radio show when he was younger, worked in college at a radio station, and followed the trends in the radio business. His dream was to become a DJ, something he never gave up on. In his mid-70s, he went over to his local radio station, hung out there, made friends with the personnel, and volunteered as a go-fer. He was asked to do some research, and eventually, when the station was in a bind, he had to read some copy on air. He then catapulted himself into his own career as a DJ.

Here's a list of dreams people have shared with us:

- Start my own business
- Start a chartered sailing business
- Design a line of clothing
- Walk across the 17 bridges in Manhattan
- Go back to school to become a shrink
- Become a volunteer for AmeriCorps
- Open a bed and breakfast
- Invent a new product
- Teach at a college
- Start a tennis league
- Write the Great American Novel
- Go around the world in 80 days
- Cut a demo tape
- Become a dog handler
- Run for office

We believe you can achieve your dream if you're flexible, proactive, and positive. But you first have to get it out of your head and into the realm of possibility. Writing it down is the critical first step.

Pursuing Your Interests

Rewiring offers people the chance to focus on their current and deferred interests. Some people pursue an interest their whole lives, continuing with it at retirement time. Some even turn avocations into vocations.

Ron, a retired physicist, mathematician, and computational scientist, has had a lifelong interest in the theater, first in college and then during his professional years in amateur community theater. He is now the managing director of Theater Three in Port Jefferson, New York, receiving a small salary. "We offer far from a living wage," he says, "but you get to be part of a great community, with activity, people, enjoyment, and pleasure. It's wonderful for retired people."[3]

Nick, a retiree we interviewed, turned his lifelong interest in photography into a rewired vocation as a freelance photographer for the local paper.

An interest can also be something that's been dormant for a long time. For example, Jane and Hank have been married for almost 40 years. He is a retired jeweler. She is a retired child psychologist. They are both artistically talented but only dabbled in the arts during most of their professional lives as they raised a family. When they retired, they launched their retirement with a three-week stint in Tuscany. Jane packed a set of watercolors, pastels, and paper, and their jaunt through the hills ignited their artistic fever. In retirement, they have focused on artistic endeavors and do very different but related work. They have just completed their fourth art show, where they sold more than 68 percent of their work.

When Frank, a 68-year-old bond trader, left his company, he took a different route. He decided to look back into his past to figure out what to do. "I want to finish what I started years ago," he told us. He explained that under pressure from his family he switched from a Master's in history to getting his MBA. "I wanted to finish my history Master's," he explained. "By the time I finish, I'm going to be 70. But heck, I'm going to be 70 anyway." Rewiring can be the time to "complete a major incompletion," as our friend and nonfinancial retirement counselor, Anita Lands, says.

Tip

Beyond your own drivers, think about the importance of having interests that keep you mentally stimulated for your own health. Medical research indicates that keeping yourself mentally stimulated can stave off aging as well as diseases such as Alzheimer's. So as you think about your interests, you might want to consider learning how to play bridge, taking up a language, or doing crossword puzzles—three interests in particular doctors recommended for keeping your brain active.

Making New Discoveries

Rewiring is the time to make new discoveries. If you keep an open mind, discoveries can even become rewired careers. George, 58, retired after 30 years as an engineer for the U.S. Navy. He wanted to stay active but wasn't sure what he should do, so he took a vocational aptitude exam at a local community college and, to his surprise, scored high for applied arts— something he had never thought of doing. He went to school and got his Associate's degree in graphic design. Now, at 63, he telecommutes 20 to 40 hours a week for a consulting firm. "I feel like I've died and gone to heaven," he says. "I love it. I can't get enough."[4] If you keep your eyes open, discoveries will land in your lap. For example, Jimmy and Rosalynn Carter discovered bird watching coincidentally in their retirement years while climbing Mt. Kilimanjaro. The Carters now spend many pleasurable hours in retirement watching birds no matter where they are, even in their own backyard.[5]

Tip

Looking for ways to uncover your interests? Read course listings in catalogues from community and other colleges, the YWCA, The Learning Annex, Discovery Center, and adult education courses. (Your public library often has these.) Or check out the offerings of the more than 300 learning in retirement programs, most of which are affiliated with colleges. Keyword search "learning in retirement" in your favorite search engine.

Thought Starters on Interests and Discoveries

Do you need some thought starters on how to discover what interests you? The Internet, whether it's at home or the library, makes finding interests easier than ever. Go to the home page of a major portal, such as yahoo.com. There you'll find clubs, or groups, under the keywords "hobbies and crafts." You can also go to google.com and keyword search for a particular interest. If you aren't sure what you're interested in, you can browse lists of hobbies online, too. A keyword search of "hobbies" will turn up many listings of hobbies, which you can look through at your leisure. For example, Yahoo! has an excellent A to Z listing of hobbies at dir.groups.yahoo.com/dir/Hobbies___Crafts/Hobbies.

Ten Steps to Exploring an Interest

Whether you have an interest you want to deepen or an interest you don't know a thing about and are looking for a way to get started, here are 10 steps to exploring it:

1. Write a sentence that defines what your interest is.
2. Ask yourself how this interest began and why it's important to you. (When did it start? Was it a sudden event, or did it develop over time? Did someone inspire you to learn more?)
3. Outline what you have done up to now to learn more about the subject.
4. What would you like to achieve with this interest? Think about what goals you can set for yourself (e.g., become an expert, be very proficient or be knowledgeable about the subject, be a participant in activities pertaining to the subject, meet new people who share the interest, and so on).
5. Who else do you know of who shares your interest? You might already be acquainted with this person, or you might want to get to know this person.
6. What clubs, organizations, or groups that focus on this interest could you join or become associated with?

continues

continued

Ten Steps to Exploring an Interest

7. Who are the experts or professionals who are recognized in this area of interest? (They may be national, regional, or local figures who are prominent in the subject.)
8. How could you contact or network to meet the experts?
9. What other things could you do to get more immersed in the subject?
10. Don't be afraid to discard. Remember, if you get into something and it's not right for you, move on.

Real People: Susan

For Susan, 62, food has always been an interest. A former children's book editor, she joked that she really couldn't see how food could play a part in her retirement but admitted that since she was a child, she had loved everything to do with exotic cooking. Her grandmother, who had lived with her and her parents, had been very adventuresome and had cooked special meals from many different cultures with Susan when she was a girl. To this day, Susan always asks chefs at ethnic restaurants for recipes she likes. Susan thought that if she had more time she might become a real chef.

Susan used the preceding "Ten Steps to Exploring an Interest" and our help to begin spinning out ideas:

➡ Immerse herself in the culture of the country and its food, and write about it.

➡ Start a local cooking club where she could teach. (Many of her friends are not great cooks but had all expressed a desire to learn more sophisticated culinary techniques.)

➡ Teach a basic class for beginners at the local college.

➡ Teach her friends' daughters and sons how to cook.

➡ Take cooking classes in the United States or abroad.

➡ Work as a kitchen helper at a restaurant or a caterer to learn food preparation.

➡ Cater. (Susan isn't sure she wants the responsibility of running a business, though.)

➡ Freelance for a food magazine, or even start an online food newsletter.

➡ Start a TV food show. She knows people at her local TV station who might be able to help.

➡ Do food demonstrations at local retail stores, such as A&P or Whole Foods.

➡ Become a nutritionist. She could enroll at her local college to become a nutritionist or do something else in the food sciences area.

➡ Run a restaurant in partnership with a restaurant owner.

➡ Sell food products she manufactures. Could she sell favorite recipes at local markets, à la Paul Newman brands?

➡ Work in sales at the local Williams-Sonoma store.

➡ Write a kids' book that has to do with food.

➡ Do public relations work for the food industry, beginning pro bono until she establishes her credibility.

➡ Write a restaurant review column for her local newspaper.

Tip

Remember to check your dreams against your drivers. You'll see how interests stack up against drivers and other considerations in later chapters.

Still stumped? The following box, provided by our friend Anita Lands, offers more thought starters. Again, as you jot down your answers, know why you've answered as you have. "The *why* is critical," says Anita.

Twenty Questions to Identify Interests

1. Which movies do you enjoy most? Why?
2. What television programs do you find interesting? Why?
3. If you were asked to create a TV special, what would it be about?
4. What part of the newspaper do you read? Why?
5. What magazines intrigue you most at newsstands? Why?
6. What would you like to write a book about? Why?
7. What were your favorite books from the past two years? What interests do they reflect?
8. What subjects did you enjoy most in any educational setting?
9. What subjects would you like to learn about now? Go back to school for?
10. How would you use a gift of $10 million?
11. What current leisure activities do you engage in?
12. What have you thought about doing over the last few months?
13. How would you spend a month of vacation right now?
14. What kinds of places do you visit or think about often? Why?
15. If you started a small business, what would it be?
16. Is there anything you believe in so strongly that you would work at it full-time for no salary?
17. If you were given several free hours to talk to an "interesting" person of your choice (real or imaginary), describe whom you would choose.
18. Among celebrities or famous people (dead or alive), whom do you find interesting? What qualities make them interesting to you?
19. What organization would you volunteer at? Give money to?
20. What issue is important enough to you that you would devote time and effort to it as a "cause"?

Establishing Your Legacy

A final way to get at your dreams is to search for your deepest values—your beliefs about what you feel is important in life. If you follow your deeply held beliefs, it can make the difference between a life that's meaningful and a life that isn't. The next step is to ask yourself what you want your life to stand for—what you want to have accomplished in this world before you die. When you ask what you want to leave behind after you're gone, you're dealing with legacy questions. Take the following legacy quiz to find out. Jot down your answers.

Legacy Quiz

Imagine your funeral. Who will attend? Who do you want to deliver your eulogy? What would you like that person to say? What would you like your obituary to say? How would you like to be remembered by others in your town or community?

To what extent are you involved in activities *now* that are part of your legacy? Write down your answers. It doesn't take that much to leave something of value. It only takes $10,000 to start a family foundation, for example. And lots of other kinds of legacies exist. You may want to pass social values to the next generation, for example, by getting your grandchildren involved in volunteerism, or doing a family tree genealogy project, or making an audio record of your life's history. You may want to write an inspirational book on overcoming challenges, start a lobbying initiative in your state capitol, power up your business so you can leave it to your kids, or be a player in national politics. These are all examples of legacy activities.

Without dreams, life isn't worth living. If you can't work your dreams in right now, start today to include them in your rewired life at retirement time.

Real Quotes

I wouldn't have focused on photography if it weren't for an off-hand comment a friend made one day. "You're good at photography." I listened.
—Nick, 70

The Top Four Dream Stealers

If you've taken a look at your dreams, interests, and discoveries and you're still hesitating, what's holding you back? Your attitude. If you're like most people, what you think about your dreams is as important as the dreams themselves. Your attitude can make it possible for you to achieve your dreams, or it can keep you from achieving them. In other words, if you think you can't have your dreams, you're right!

We call negative thoughts *dream stealers*. Dream stealers center on problems in a narrow, negative way that keeps you from solving the problems creatively. Dream stealers make you think of all the reasons *why you can't* do something, instead of *how you can.* The following sections ID the top four dream stealers. Do you recognize your thoughts in any of them?

Dream Stealer #1: "I Can't Afford It"

Money is a great excuse. A lot of people get so hung up on money that they don't even give their dreams a chance. So the first thing we suggest is to answer the question *How can I tell if money is keeping me from my dreams?* Here's the good news, though: you can have your dream without breaking the bank.

Write down your dream(s) identified earlier in the chapter. *How much does your dream really cost?* To help you figure that out, weigh the dream in terms of dollars and cents. What does the experience cost (in terms of dollars and/or time), and how does the cost stack up against what you expect to get from the experience? What will you need to lay out in money, hours of your time, or other resources versus what you will get from that

experience? Use all the five senses to describe the experience—
sight, smell, sound, taste, and touch. What's the cost? Write your
answers.

If you decide in terms of dollars and cents that the dream
isn't worth it, it's time to go back to the drawing board. You have
to figure out if you can have the dream in levels, with accompanying levels of expenditures. Ask yourself, *What can I afford
that's close to my dream?* Think about what costs a lot. What costs
a medium amount of money, a little bit of money? It's often possible to have the dream without the highest price tag. It doesn't
have to be all or nothing.

Tip

Dreams come with price tags. Remember to figure in the costs
of projects you'll pursue. Board seats and other nonprofit committee work often require a financial contribution. The costs of
hobbies such as painting, photography, or even crafts can also
add up.

Jill, 50, is a medical lab technician in Pittsburgh. She has
always had an interest in the Civil War and would love to leave
medicine behind when she retires. She loves to visit Civil War
battlefields and dreams about finding a way to immerse herself
in the Civil War, to live it daily. She found out that the Park
Service has a program where you can lease property on the
grounds of the Civil War battlefields. Her dream is to run a B&B
on one of the battlefields or a related site. Her husband, a restaurant owner, would like to open a nearby restaurant. Jill isn't
sure if her dream is worth it in terms of dollars and cents. If
she and her husband decide they can't afford the B&B and the
restaurant, Jill may get involved in Civil War battle reenactment.
She has recently learned that more than 30,000 people come
dressed in authentic period costumes to reenact the Battle of
Gettysburg every July. That sounds like a way for her to live and
breathe the Civil War in a way that may make dollars and cents
to her. She decides to start getting involved now.

Dream Stealer #2: "I Don't Know How"

Let's say your dream is to collect antique toys. But you don't know a thing about them, and nobody else you know does, either. What do you do? How do you start to get into something that has no connection whatsoever to your life?

In fact, it's easier than ever today to open up a new world of interest because you can get so much information on the Internet. Although we still recommend talking to real human beings for most of your investigating, the best place to start is online. When you want to talk to real people, one of the best ways is to find an association. There's an association for almost everything today. To find the association, go to google.com (or another search engine) and do a keyword search. Your public librarians can also help you find associations that match your interests.

Once you've found an appropriate organization, contact someone at the club or association. Explain that you'd like to learn more, and ask what they recommend. Maybe they'll refer you to antique shows, flea markets, antique newspapers and magazines, even eBay and *Antiques Roadshow*. Get on their mailing list. Attend their meetings, or ask if you can attend meetings on a trial basis. Become a member. Talk to officers of the association who can answer your questions.

When it comes to exploring an interest, there's one important lesson to remember: it's okay to show your naïveté, to be an absolute beginner. You were born knowing absolutely nothing and you survived. Not only that, every person in your life was a stranger to you when you first met. So it's okay to know nothing and no one. All you have to do is ask for help along the way.

Real Quotes

He who asks a question is a fool for five minutes. He who does not ask a question remains a fool forever.
—Chinese proverb

Dream Stealer #3: "What If I Fail?"

A dream involves risk. When you've laid your cards on the table and declared your dream, what if it doesn't work out? You've stuck your neck out in plain sight for everyone to see. How will you look?

This type of fear, the fear of failure, keeps a lot of people from achieving their dreams. Jim, 58, is a talented character actor who is in the fortunate situation of having been employed for most of his career. He has a wonderful idea for a rewired post-retirement career. He has always had an interest in General George Patton and views him as a role model. Jim has worked up a 45-minute presentation in character as General Patton in full regalia. He's thinking about rewiring and offering a one-man inspirational General Patton lecture and tour around the country. Europeans find Patton interesting, and Jim's even thinking about touring in Europe.

Jim has spoken to members of a business roundtable group in Philadelphia (where he lives) about doing gigs there, has contacted speaker's bureaus, and has even approached schools. But as he's gotten closer to giving it the green light, everything comes to a halt. Jim keeps asking himself, *What if it doesn't work? How will I look?* Jim is afraid of failure.

If your fear of failure is holding you back from your dreams, imagine the worst by following these steps:

1. Ask yourself what your worst fear is.
2. Now imagine that what you fear the most has already happened. Whose reactions do you fear the most? Imagine what their reactions will be.
3. How do you react once the worst has happened?

Now that your reactions and everyone else's are on the table, was it as bad as you anticipated? Was your worst fear as bad as you thought it would be? Or better? Did people react as badly as you thought they would, or were they supportive? Do you care?

Anticipating the worst is a way to address your fears ahead of time and work through whether the dream is worth pursuing or not.

Dream Stealer #4: "What If She/He Hates It?"

Let's say you've declared your dream and your spouse or significant other hates it. Although we've said all along your dream is for *you*, the truth is, you don't exist in a vacuum. You have important relationships that you're committed to, including possibly a spouse, significant other, or family members who rely on you. Many people change or postpone their dreams when their dreams cause conflict with loved ones. But it doesn't have to be that way.

Many conflicts can be sorted out with communication and compromise. For example, one man we know wanted to move out of Chicago after being forced into retirement from a Chicago firm at age 67. His wife, who was very active in philanthropic work in Chicago, was stunned. They worked out a compromise. She went along with the idea, although she wasn't a happy camper. Through a connection, he set up an opportunity to go to England for a year. In England, his wife continued to keep up her Chicago connections. When she came back, she just picked up right where she left off. He came back with an English project to complete in the United States, some good stories, and a sense of having saved face. The best tactic is communication, communication, communication. Remember: don't squelch yourself. The more honest you can be when you negotiate with loved ones, the better.

If you find yourself trapped by these dream stealers, look for creative solutions. A dream is like a jewel that's beautiful from one angle, but also from many others. The trick is to look at the jewel from different angles. If you hold your dream in your hand and turn it, and turn it, and turn it, you can often find a way to bring its beauty into your life.

The Four Pre-Retirees

At this point, it's time to check in again with our four pre-retirees. What are their dreams and interests? We'll come back to their dreams and interests as we watch them *rewire* throughout the rest of the book.

Tom

Tom is the national sales director who's looking at retirement in six months.

Dream: to play golf all year round

Interests: sports, coaching, theater, cards

Drivers:

> #5 Competition—to be competitive
>
> #12 Goals—to have and to share goals
>
> #18 Mentoring—to mentor others
>
> #27 Social—to be connected to others
>
> #28 Structure—to have structure

Paula

Paula owns an HR consulting business and is nuts about sailing. She was a foster child and supports initiatives for young girls and women.

Dream: to sail around the world and to leave some type of legacy

Interests: sailing; women's, adolescents', and societal issues

Drivers:

> #8 Experiences—to have new experiences
>
> #14 Intellectual Stimulation—to be with intellectually stimulating people
>
> #23 Problem-Solving—to be a problem-solver
>
> #29 Value—to give value to others or to be valued
>
> #30 Visibility—to have visibility

Bob

Bob is the engineer who works at a major automotive manufacturer and runs the firm's community outreach activities. He's very active in his church.

Dream: to caretake a World War I cemetery in France

Interests: World War I history, community and church activities

Drivers:

> #3 Authority—to be an authority figure
>
> #4 Belonging—to have a sense of belonging
>
> #16 Lifelong Learning—to be constantly learning
>
> #17 Making a Difference—to help make the world better
>
> #24 Recognition—to be recognized

Carol

Carol was on Wall Street and has an extensive network of social, political, and business contacts.

Dream: to make life better for animals in the United States and around the world

Interests: animals, politics, fund-raising, art, travel

Drivers:

> #2 Action—to be "part of the action"
>
> #10 Fulfillment—to be fulfilled
>
> #13 Identity—to have an identity
>
> #17 Making a Difference—to help make the world better
>
> #20 People—to have exposure to people

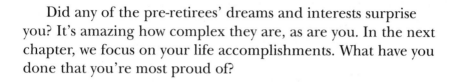

Real Quotes

If something is boring you, it is probably you.
—Roger Rosenblatt[6]

Did any of the pre-retirees' dreams and interests surprise you? It's amazing how complex they are, as are you. In the next chapter, we focus on your life accomplishments. What have you done that you're most proud of?

Chapter 8
Own Your Accomplishments

I'm ninety-one and still practicing law and have no intention of stopping.
—*Phillip, 91*

The happiest rewirees are people who have cast their nets wide, dreamed big, and acknowledged who they are and what they "own." You may have grown a prize-winning rose, gotten promoted to vice president, raised wonderful children, or hiked the Great Wall of China. You *own* these life accomplishments—they're *yours,* and the strengths and skills associated with them are part of your life toolbox.

Knowing what you accomplished in the past and found satisfying is important because it can lead you to similar satisfying activities in the future. Moreover, the strengths and skills you used to bring about your life accomplishments are transferable—you take them with you into your rewired life, anywhere you want, doing anything you want. You can also choose not to use any skill you no longer want to use when you *rewire.*

Peeling the Artichoke

In this chapter, you'll list your accomplishments and the strengths and skills you used to achieve them. This is not the standard skills assessment you may have done in the past. We assume you know your skills, but you probably haven't thought about which ones you want to continue using, develop, or put on hold when you *rewire*. The process of analyzing your accomplishments this way is a lot like peeling an artichoke down to get to its heart. You'll answer five questions:

➡ What are my top 10 life accomplishments?

➡ What drivers did my accomplishments fulfill?

➡ What strengths or skills did I use to achieve my accomplishments?

➡ Which of these strengths or skills do I want to use when I *rewire*? Which skills do I want to add?

➡ Which of these strengths or skills do I want to table?

Real Quotes

Am I going to let what is going on in the world out there determine who I am and what I do? Or am I going to let what's going on inside of me, in terms of my enthusiasms, my interests, my skills, my values and my beliefs, determine who I am and what I do?

—Richard Nelson Bolles, author of *What Color Is Your Parachute?*[1]

Your Top Ten Accomplishments

In this section you'll identify your top 10 accomplishments. Ask yourself these questions to get started:

➡ What am I most proud of having accomplished?

➡ What goals did I complete and feel good about?

➡ What do I brag about to myself or others?

Jot down any answers to these questions. As you identify your accomplishments, keep these pointers in mind:

➡ Don't limit your list to your professional life only.

➡ Think about your entire life: personal, professional, family, spiritual, leisure and travel, formal learning, community, sports and outdoor activities, hobbies and crafts, home, etc.

➡ Don't consider what other people think—it doesn't matter. Remember, you're going for only one nirvana—yours.

➡ Try to limit your list to 10 accomplishments, but it's okay if you have more.

Coming up with life accomplishments is about taking into account all the complexity and individuality of each of our lives. Don't get into the trap of setting the bar too high. Give yourself credit for what you've achieved. You don't have to be on the Supreme Court to be proud of what you've done. And don't minimize or negate your accomplishments. There will be those who say, "That was no big deal about backpacking the Appalachian Trail." But it is a big deal if it's a big deal to you. Paint with broad brushstrokes, and don't rate your accomplishments against someone else's criteria. You're not doing this exercise to be competitive; you're trying to get to the heart of the matter—your life.

We've included examples of life accomplishments in the following box. These are real-life examples, offered by retirees and pre-retirees in our focus groups when we asked them to tell us which of their life accomplishments they were most proud of. When you look at the list, you'll notice that it includes all kinds of items, big and small, professional and personal. Take a look at the list to get your own ideas started.

Examples of Life Accomplishments

Delivered a great speech and got a standing ovation.

Won a sales contest three years in a row.

Discovered and implemented new software for the company to use, which saved a fortune.

Worked with others to start our town's first high-school hockey team.

Increased efficacy of a product through persistence and testing.

Cared for my mother before she died.

Created a unique integrated marketing campaign.

Hiked the Great Wall of China.

Lowered my golf handicap from 15 to 8.

Sold the most Girl Scout cookies in my troop's history.

Quit drinking.

Created several strategic alliances with organizations in Asia.

Created a great mentoring program for my company.

Raised wonderful children.

Left New York City and moved to Montana.

Left Montana and moved to New York City.

Grew my business 121 percent over 3 years.

Grew a prize-winning rose.

Backpacked the Appalachian Trail.

Kept staff motivated at the company at a critical time.

Hired great people who took us to new heights.

Was recognized by the president for being a major fund-raiser for the party.

Lived in another culture.

Designed a great floor plan for an architectural project.

Wrote and sold my first novel.

Analyzed financial numbers and caught a major reporting problem.

Patented a product.

Stopped a mugging.

Calmed a patient's nerves.

Took the mule ride to the bottom of the Grand Canyon.

Won a major lawsuit against a major city government.

Got on *The New York Times* bestseller list.

Gave the commencement address at my alma mater.

Learned to fly a plane.

Slept in the Lincoln bedroom.

Lost 20 pounds and kept it off.

Saved the company millions through the creation of a shared-services department.

Biked through Europe.

Helped a client solve a major human resources problem.

Saved my sister from drowning.

Played a femme fatale in a community theater production.

Learned a new language.

Always had a positive attitude, even in the face of danger.

Never let others see me sweat.

Visited every major league baseball stadium on summer vacations with my family.

Reengineered a division.

Visited a sick friend often.

Increased diversity numbers for the company.

Broke more accounts than had ever been done before.

Discovered a new delivery system for prescription drugs.

Saved people money through tax planning.

Played in the Masters in Augusta.

Adopted twins.

Created my own definition of success.

Was named an "up and comer" by a national magazine.

Ran for office and won.

Learned to paint after the age of 40.

Got over my fear of flying.

Made it through some tough marital times.

Graduated Phi Beta Kappa.

continues

continued

Examples of Life Accomplishments

Raised more than a million dollars for a charity.

Overcame my fear of animals.

Mentored people who got promoted as a result.

Made a difference at my church.

Captained the baseball team in college.

Got my own segment on TV.

Saved an innocent man from going to jail.

Learned to cook.

Beat cancer.

Earned Eagle Scout.

Started my own company.

Set a sports record in college.

Stopped worrying about what others thought of me.

Was asked to join a prestigious country club.

Trained for the Iron Man competition.

Invented a new piece of equipment.

Became recognized as the person who could fix problems.

Got out of the market before the bubble burst.

Bet on the right horse at the Derby and won.

Put eight kids through college.

Got myself out of bankruptcy.

Rode a horse.

Your Top Ten

Now that you've reviewed the list, it's your turn to identify your top 10 accomplishments. You can see that the people we interviewed used broad brushstrokes. If this exercise is familiar to you, remember that this time you're doing it for a different reason—to see what accomplishments really got you charged up and that you'd like to have more of in the future.

As a starter, we tell clients to think back over their lives in five-year increments. Don't try to tackle your whole life in one fell swoop. What did you accomplish that you're proud of at work? At leisure? Think sports, family, church, organizations, community, friends. What comes up? Can you take credit for anything similar to the accomplishments in the preceding list? Write down your answers. Some people can't stop writing; others find it hard to begin. No matter what, don't set the bar too high.

Did you have more than 10? If so, rank them according to what you really got the most charge out of, and pare down the list to only 10. Ten should give you a good breadth of your achievements.

 Real Quotes

If we wish to have the brightest of futures, we need to know the best of our pasts.

—Toni Morrison

Reality Check

How many of your top 10 accomplishments fulfill drivers? Review your list of drivers to see. Was it one out of ten? Five out of ten? All ten? What kind of accomplishments did you have? What categories did they fall under? Were they related to sports, community, family, work, or personal? Were they in one area more predominantly than others? If your accomplishments are all work-related, you're going to need to add more interests, hobbies, or leisure into your rewired life—or else keep working!

If you felt happy, elated, pumped up, or satisfied when you looked at your top 10 list, we're willing to bet that at least some of your drivers were fulfilled through your accomplishments. Taking an example from the preceding box, "saving an innocent man from going to jail" could be the fulfillment of the making a difference driver. Depending on the person, "inventing a new piece of equipment" could be the fulfillment of several drivers, including accomplishments, competition, creativity, intellectual stimulation, lifelong learning, passion, problem-solving, recognition, skills and talent, or value. The squash club champ who holds the club title may fulfill his competition, belonging, recognition, visibility, and identity drivers.

Some of our accomplishments don't fulfill a specific driver but are in line with our personal values and beliefs. For example, raising good children can be a reflection of your strongly held values about the importance of family. As we've said elsewhere, when you *rewire*, you'll want to think about how to have activities that bring driver fulfillment into your new life. We now add that you should also think about your life accomplishments as another guide.

The Halo Effect

Life accomplishments have a halo effect. They impress people, and telling others about them is pleasurable. Without their social dividends, many people wouldn't accomplish as much as they do. Think of all the people who have told you about a life accomplishment soon after you met them or were getting to know them. These accomplishments run the gamut from catching a record-setting fish, to fighting Rommel with the Allies in North Africa in World War II, to volunteering every week in the children's hospital for more than 20 years, to trekking in the Himalayas.

Which of your top 10 do you like to share with others?

Things to Think About

Here are some additional questions to ask yourself about your top 10 list. Jot down your answers.

➡ Which audiences or social groups were involved in accomplishing my top 10?

➡ What kinds of applause did my top 10 provide?

➡ What feelings relating to the top 10, if any, would I like to recapture?

➡ Do I want to continue to get that feeling when I rewire?

See if you can think of the accomplishment in generic terms, as a type of accomplishment, not just as the literal accomplishment itself. What is it about the accomplishment that turned you on? Break it down into the audience and the environment. For example, you may have found it fulfilling to work on creative projects with people you like. As an advertising copywriter, for example, you enjoyed being part of a creative team that did cutting-edge campaigns. You may be able to transfer that driver fulfillment to a new organization and a new group of people when you *rewire* by planning and executing the publicity and marketing for a local theater group.

If giving speeches at work gave you the chance for visibility and you want to continue to fulfill that driver when you *rewire,* you might want to give speeches for Chamber of Commerce audiences or through Toastmasters.

Strengths and Skills

Your top 10 accomplishments happened because of your strengths and skills, as well as your drivers. Knowing your skills is important because you need to know what you have to offer and what you want to offer.

There remains a lot of controversy about strengths versus skills and about how much is innate versus how much is learned. There's no way we can settle this widespread cultural debate in this book, and we won't even try. The most practical and useful way to look at it is that strengths are innate and skills are learned. We add one qualifier to keep in mind: your strengths and skills may be brought out in different ways in different situations. For example, you may have life skills that aren't used on the job and vice versa. The same goes for strengths. Your wisdom may not be utilized on the job as much as at home. And a lot depends on you; you have a lot of control. How do you want to use your strengths and skills?

Strengths are what you have to work with; skills are what you develop.

Tip

If you match your skills perfectly to the task you're engaged in, you're likely to become completely absorbed. This pleasurable state of mind is what Mihaly Csikszentmihalyi calls "flow," a feeling of such engagement and focus that time seems to pass unnoticed.

Taking Your Strengths and Skills into the Future

You've been living with your strengths and skills a long time and you have a lot of them. If you know them right off the top of your head, great. But if you don't, to make it easier for you to identify them, look at your top 10 accomplishments identified earlier and see what it took to achieve them. Let's say, for example, that you climbed Mount Everest. It wasn't just your competition driver that enabled you to accomplish the feat. You also had a set of strengths, including athletic ability, endurance, physical strength, and good balance. Your skills may have included the ability to plan an expedition, marshal the resources, and analyze and problem-solve all the issues involved in coordinating and equipping yourself or a team, not to mention executing myriad highly skilled climbing tasks—some large, some small.

We're not asking you to do a plain-vanilla skills inventory here. You've no doubt done that many times. We want you to focus forward: which of these strengths and skills do you like enough to use when you *rewire*?

Look at the following list of strengths and skills, and ask yourself which of these (and any others) you used to accomplish your top 10. The lists are not meant to be complete, but they are intended to get you thinking. (If you have a strength that's important to you that isn't related to one of your top 10 accomplishments, don't exclude it.) Write down your answers. A few examples include the following:

Selected strengths:

Ambitious	Hard-working
Analytical	Honest
Athletic	Inspirational
Balanced	Logical
Caring	Looks the part
Cause-driven	Maintains a presence
Charismatic	Mentorable
Confident	Open-minded/fair
Connector of people	Optimistic
Creative	Passionate
Determined	Patient
Direct	Perceptive
Enthusiastic	Persistent
Entrepreneurial	Results-oriented
Ethical	Risk-oriented
Friendly	Self-motivated
Goal-oriented	Sense of humor
Good attitude	Sensitive to others' needs
Good values	Smart

Spiritual	Thoughtful
Strategic	Tough
Take-charge personality	Trustworthy
Takes responsibility	Values diversity
Team player	Wise
Thorough/well prepared	*(Any others)*

Now that you've written down your strengths, it's time to look at your skills. Look at the following list of selected skills. Which skills listed here (as well as any others you may add) did you use to accomplish your top 10? Write down your answers.

Selected skills:

Acting	Decision-making
Adapting	Delegating
Analyzing	Delivering the goods
Artistic skill	Developing
Assessing a situation	Empowering
Athletic skills	Financial managing
Building/creating	Focusing
Caretaking	Fund-raising
Closing	Growing
Communicating	Handling situations
Computers	Independent thinking
Consensus-building	Industry-specific knowledge
Constructing	Internet
Counseling	Interpersonal skills
Critiquing	Languages/translating
Culinary	skills

Leading

Listening

Managing people

Marketing/self-marketing

Mechanical

Mediating

Mentoring

Motivating others

Negotiating

Networking

Numerical skills

Overcoming obstacles

Painting

Paying attention to details

Performing

Planning/organizing

Politicking

Presenting

Preserving

Prioritizing

Problem-solving

Project/task skills

Public speaking

Researching/data gathering

Restoring

Scientific/technical skills

Self-promoting

Selling/persuading

Socializing

Strategizing

Teaching/instructing

Team/alliance-building

Technical skills

Theatrical skills

Thinking/outside-the-box thinking

Training

Transporting (driving, flying, sailing)

Vision/envisioning

Visual

Writing

(Any others)

What did you write as your list of skills you used to accomplish your top 10? Look over your list and identify the strengths and skills you "own." We know you assessed your skills when you wrote your resumé or CV, but you're doing this now with a new eye toward what you really want to do in your rewired life, not what others want you to do.

Looking into your history from a strengths and skills standpoint should put a smile on your face, and you should feel that you have a lot of valuable strengths and skills to use when you *rewire*, if you choose to. Some might have been dormant and just haven't been used in a while. You may choose to further develop other skills in *rewirement*, but first you must recognize the ones you already own.

Rewiring with Your Strengths and Skills

Just because you're good at a certain skill doesn't mean you want to use it when you *rewire*. For example, Francine, 72, was good at numbers and had been a budget analyst during her career, but she didn't want to have anything to do with calculations when she rewired. Instead, she chose to volunteer at her local soup kitchen and teach yoga at the local YWCA.

Boards or other organizations might want to tap you for your skills. Don't get caught in a trap of saying "yes" just because you're asked. They may want something from you that you no longer want to use. On the other hand, you can also use your skills to get you in the door and parlay that into broader opportunities you really want.

Adapting or Adding

We all have talents we've never used or haven't used in a while. That's why it's important to know our strengths and skills inside and out. In this section, we look at how you can enhance, adapt, or otherwise change how you use your skills to gain more driver fulfillment in your rewired life. For example, Mike, 57, retired after 30 years of teaching. He had loved teaching high school science but was tired of collecting, researching, and imparting theoretical information in a way that had little impact on students' lives. He wanted to have a personal impact on individuals' lives.

Mike decided to add a new skill—counseling—in his rewired career and got a Master's degree in social work. He focused on family counseling with an emphasis on crisis counseling. In his rewired work, he still imparted knowledge and used many of his same strengths and skills that he used when he was a teacher, but his audience and his role in the process had changed. Working one-on-one with families, he was no longer imparting knowledge that was going to be used in a theoretical, impersonal way, but rather knowledge that had a real impact on the families he was working with. He was much happier in his rewired career because he knew that in sharing the information this way, he was making a difference and being of value, two of his most important drivers.

After a long career, you might want to adapt your skills in a related career that uses similar skills. That's what Anne Baley did. Anne, 67, worked as a missionary doctor for more than 20 years in Zambia. In the early 1980s, as associate professor of medicine at the university teaching hospital in Lusaka, the capital, she realized that patients she was seeing in the clinic had AIDS, something only a few doctors in Africa realized at the time. As she continued to care for sick and dying patients, she remembered her childhood desire to join the ministry. "I was dealing often— well, all the time—with people who were facing the ultimate questions of death and dying," she said. In 1990, she left Zambia for theological training in England, and she was ordained an Anglican priest in 1994.[2]

Which strengths or skills do you want to adapt when you *rewire?* You can use existing skills and adapt them to start a business. Caroline, 66, was a sculptor while her husband still worked but adapted her artistic skills at his retirement time. She now designs door pulls and sells them through her own website. Her husband, Bill, 67, has taken over the marketing of her business. They're having a ball. The new business has saved his sanity and given them a wonderful outlet to share, plus income.

You may decide to go from using business skills to using personal artistic skills. Sarah, 50, a divorced single mom, was bored in her career as a chemical engineer because (among other reasons) it didn't offer enough fulfillment for her creativity driver. She quit working when she married a widower who had already retired. She and her husband split the year between the Poconos in Pennsylvania in the summer months and Florida in the winter. Sarah is exploring painting of all types (watercolors, oil, pastels) to fulfill her accomplishment and creativity drivers. Her frustration is that her skill level is still low, but she is seeing improvement. Because painting is a portable hobby, it's especially suited to her East Coast snowbird lifestyle.

Do you have any skills you want to add or enhance when you *rewire*? Did you identify dreams or interests in Chapter 7 that require new skills? Don't discard a dream just because you don't have the necessary skills. If the desire is there, the "how" will emerge. Write them down. You can use Chapter 7's methods for developing interests to develop your skills as well.

Back Burner Your Skills

All of us are good at things we're not wild about doing. So when it comes time to *rewire*, many people decide to focus on skills they really love or want to develop and back burner the rest. Many people want to focus on new experiences, novelty things they've always dreamed of doing and being—definitely not just the same old thing! In a ritual of back burnering, Sarah, the aforementioned chemical engineer, threw out her engineering reference books when she quit working. She saw that as a form of commitment to her new life.

Which strengths, skills, or situations do you want to steer away from when you *rewire*? They may be job-related, or they could be situations you don't want to be placed in, using skills you don't want to use. Look back over the list of skills you created earlier in the chapter and also review the following list of workplace situations to get ideas. Jot down anything you want to table. You might wonder why we're asking you to do this. Rewiring is a time of opportunity, and it's your time to create a great next act. So admit what you don't want to take forward with you.

Rewirees told us they had been skillful at managing the following workplace situations, but that these were the kinds of things they wanted to steer away from if they could in their future:

➡ Back-stabbing associates

➡ Bad bosses

➡ Being beholden to a boss

➡ Being on call

➡ Being on time

➡ Boredom

➡ Commuting

➡ Egos

➡ Getting up early

➡ Having a boss

➡ Having face-time with clients

➡ Having to do what other people want you to do

➡ Having to pretend to like people you can't stand

➡ Hectic, demanding scheduling

➡ High stress levels

➡ Lack of control

➡ Lack of decision-making

➡ Living within a bureaucracy

➡ Meeting tight deadlines

➡ Meetings

➡ Office politics

➡ Participating in office politics

➡ Pressure

➡ Reporting to an idiot

➡ Traveling/being a road warrior

➡ Wearing a tie

➡ Working in teams

➡ Working on weekends

Of course, some of these things will never go away. But it's important to know what you absolutely won't do again. Al hated office politics and liked closure and getting things done. When he retired, he was asked to sit on a board. In his desire to fulfill his drivers (structure, belonging, and recognition), he accepted the position before he did his homework, and he told us he had joined a "hornet's nest." He was in an especially tough position because he wanted to honor his three-year commitment but found himself counting the days until his three years were up.

Maybe you were successful because you played office politics well. But you never valued the play, only knew you had to do it and did it well. As you craft your future, you don't want to do it anymore. Write down what you dislike.

Knowing what you don't want is almost as important as knowing what you do want in your rewired life. Add to your list anything you don't want that we've omitted. The last thing you want to do is create a rewired life full of things you dislike.

Real People: The Four Pre-Retirees

Now it's time to check in with the four pre-retirees—Carol, Bob, Paula, and Tom—and see what they've identified as their accomplishments, strengths, and skills. These are added to their drivers, dreams, and interests, to complete their personal discovery inventory, which they will use later in the book.

Tom

Tom is the national sales director who is looking at retirement in six months. He has his golf, but he also is taking a comedy class, belongs to a monthly pinochle club with his wife, and is preparing his routine to be the emcee at the golf club's members-only golf tournament dinner and at his company's upcoming sales conference.

Tom's Personal Discovery Inventory

Drivers:

> #5 Competition—to be competitive
>
> #12 Goals—to have and to share goals
>
> #18 Mentoring—to mentor others
>
> #27 Social—to be connected to others
>
> #28 Structure—to have structure

Dreams: to play golf all year round

Interests: sports, coaching, comedy, pinochle

Accomplishments:

➡ Sold an initially unknown technology service to major corporations with little advertising or marketing support

➡ Led winning sales team to achieve 1,000 percent growth in five years and was recognized for it

➡ Is asked to speak on panels frequently and keynote a major technology conference

➡ Raised two good kids and kept a great wife happy while being on the road a lot

➡ Continuously mentored new young sales execs who went on to receive promotions

➡ Current golf club champ

continues

---

continued

➡ Was asked to sit on the board of a regional theater group

➡ Played sports, on scholarship, all through college and graduated with a 3.4 average

➡ Was a part-time disc jockey for the college radio station

➡ Got the lead in high school plays three years in a row

Strengths:

Athletically inclined

Balanced

Confident

Direct

Friendly

Goal-oriented

Hard-working

Looks the part

Open-minded/fair

Sense of humor

Take-charge personality

Thorough/well prepared

Skills:

Acting skills

Asking

Athletic skills

Closing

Counseling

Developing

Handling situations

Interpersonal skills

Making it/luck happen

Managing people

Mediating

Mentoring

Presenting

Profession-specific knowledge (sales and marketing)

Selling/persuading

Socializing

When Tom looks at his list of skills, he realizes he likes who he is and the skills he owns but he's getting tired of how he has been forced to use them lately. Although he has said he wants to retire in six months because he is burned out, he is beginning to realize that he has to investigate exactly what is burning him out.

He isn't sick of selling, just sick of what, how, and to whom he is currently selling. He likes developing people, but is tired of asking them to deliver more and more. He loves challenges and being competitive but likes it to be in a healthy environment. He'd like his personality and humor, even a personal interest, to be a part of the sale. When he saw his accomplishments, he realized that he hasn't laughed a lot lately—something that was always very important to him. Tom's accomplishment analysis was really eye-opening for him.

Paula

Paula owns an HR consulting business and is nuts about sailing. She was a foster child and supports initiatives for young girls and women. She loves to go sailing with clients, her daughter, and adolescent girls, but she is also a guest lecturer (through her friends) at local universities and colleges on HR issues.

Paula's Personal Discovery Inventory

Drivers:

> #8 Experiences—to have new experiences
>
> #14 Intellectual Stimulation—to be with intellectually stimulating people
>
> #23 Problem-Solving—to be a problem-solver
>
> #29 Value—to give value to others or to be valued
>
> #30 Visibility—to have visibility

Dreams: to sail around the world and to leave some type of legacy

Interests: sailing; women's, adolescents', and foster children's issues

Accomplishments:

- Learned to sail at age 50+
- Got HR "a seat at the table" when she was an HR director at a major corporation
- Raised an outstanding daughter as a single parent
- Survived a rough childhood as a foster child
- Worked successfully with young clients even given age difference
- Brought HR benchmarking practices to emerging technology companies
- Was invited to join an exclusive business luncheon forum of senior executives and civic leaders
- Was urged by an agent to write a book on HR for non-HR types
- Was recognized for her pro bono consulting on the Children's Services Task Force

➡ Motivated a neighbor to finish her Master's degree at age 76

➡ Received high marks as a guest lecturer and speaker on HR issues and trends

Strengths:

Cause-driven

Creative

Determined

Entrepreneurial

Goal-driven

Inspirational

Maintains a presence

Perceptive

Positive attitude

Results-oriented

Smart

Skills:

Communicating

Empowering

Focusing

Marketing/self-marketing

Overcoming obstacles

Presenting

Problem-solving

Socializing

Transporting (driving, flying, sailing)

Vision/envisioning

When Paula looks at her personal discovery inventory, she recognizes that she has become a serial retiree. She loves working, but she also loves being wanted for the expertise she brings to work. She is no longer interested in the day-to-day, but she's not ready to relinquish her business role. She is conflicted about stopping work and then wonders if she should stop work or just the work she's currently doing. She's tired of the challenge of bringing in new clients.

And she is recognizing that as much as she loves sailing, the problem-solving on the water doesn't give her the same kind of charge as problem-solving on issues.

Bob

Bob is the engineer who works at a major automotive manufacturer and who runs the firm's community outreach activities. He has his WWI reading (both books and magazines), plus regular e-mailing to his Western Front Association members around the world. He's very active in his church, goes to services every Sunday, and holds a lay leadership role. He spends considerable time reading about global church issues and international missionary opportunities for couples. He is also developing a program on board governance for the nonprofit boards he's affiliated with, through work and on his own. Bob puts very high stock in work and work-related accomplishments.

Bob's Personal Discovery Inventory

Drivers:

> #3 Authority—to be an authority figure
>
> #4 Belonging—to have a sense of belonging
>
> #16 Lifelong Learning—to be constantly learning
>
> #17 Making a Difference—to help make the world better
>
> #24 Recognition—to be recognized

Dream: to caretake a World War I cemetery in France

Interests: World War I history, community and church activities

Accomplishments:

➡ Received the award for highest-performance manager of the year 20 out of 30 years, tying a company record

➡ Developed a major program in spite of bureaucratic red tape (should have taken six months, but took more than a year)

➡ Consistently kept morale high even though company went through major downsizings

➡ Offered creative technical solutions that saved the company millions of dollars and thousands of hours

➡ Represented company in major community/charitable initiatives, which included awarding funds and equipment; organizations supported have more than doubled in membership as a direct result of his efforts

➡ Built strong relationships inside the company and externally

➡ Wrote three articles to publicize volunteerism in the workplace that were published in a national magazine

➡ Celebrated 28 years of happy marriage; raised and educated three children

➡ Served as a church vestry member and warden

➡ Started a memorial scholarship to honor a co-worker who died in an accident

Strengths:

Caring

Confident

Goal-driven

Good values

continues

continued

Honest

Sensitive to the needs of others

Smart

Spiritual

Takes responsibility

Trustworthy

Skills:

Consensus-building

Decision-making

Focusing

Managing people

Prioritizing

Problem-solving

Socializing

Teaching/instructing

Team-/alliance-building

Technical skills

Values diversity

When Bob took a look at his personal discovery inventory, he realized that there were some things he liked and some things he disliked. Bob admits that he would not choose to use all these skills if he had the choice. He would quickly relinquish anything having to do with engineering but keep the logical thinking of an engineer. He would like to continue to touch lives and make a difference.

He will always be sociable and loves being part of a team, but he doesn't want the continued pressure of always living under a deadline or being called to put out fires.

Carol

Carol worked on Wall Street and has an extensive network of social, political, and business contacts. She wants to start some kind of organization to save animals. On top of her caring for her own dogs and her political interests, she attends photography exhibits, gallery openings, and modern art museums. She is an avid art catalogue browser (both printed and on the Internet).

Carol's Personal Discovery Inventory

Drivers:

> #2 Action—to be "part of the action"
>
> #10 Fulfillment—to be fulfilled
>
> #13 Identity—to have an identity
>
> #17 Making a Difference—to help make the world better
>
> #20 People—to have exposure to people

Dream: to make life better for animals in the United States and around the world

Interests: animals, politics, fund-raising, travel, modern art

Accomplishments:

➡ Raised $1 million for a candidate's political campaign

➡ Closed 10 mega-business deals in her career

➡ Went to three presidential inaugurations

➡ Raised show dogs

➡ Developed a good eye for art and photography

➡ Wrote a children's book

➡ Was elected president of her high school class

➡ Backpacked around Europe alone

continues

continued

➡ Started a small direct-mail gift business with a sorority sister after college graduation

➡ Was the number-one seller of Girl Scout cookies three years in a row

Strengths:

Ambitious

Analytical

Charismatic

Connector of people

Enthusiastic

Goal-oriented

Passionate

Risk-oriented

Self-motivated

Smart

Strategic

Tough

Wise

Skills:

Analytical skills

Asking

Assessing a situation

Building (or creating)

Communicating (speed reader)

Delivering the goods

Financial managing/bottom-line orientation

Focusing

Leadership

Planning

Socializing (can play with the big boys)

Thinking/outside-the-box thinking/brilliant thinking

Vision/envisioning

Carol reviewed her life in five-year increments to come up with her personal discovery inventory and had the following thoughts: After Carol went through the exercise of identifying her strengths and skills, she realized just how transferable her skills are from Wall Street to the development of a new nonprofit. Instead of financing deals, Carol wants to finance a new organization to save animals. She will leverage her skills to make a difference in society—saving abused animals.

Like the four pre-retirees, you need to know your strengths and skills because they enabled you to accomplish many things in your life that you're proud of, and because they are transferable into your rewired life.

Your Personal Discovery Inventory

Now it's your turn to write your own personal discovery inventory. By completing the exercises in this book, you've developed a vision. In previous chapters, you've inventoried important personal information about yourself: your drivers (Chapter 4), dreams (Chapter 7), interests (Chapters 5 and 7), accomplishments, strengths, and skills (this chapter). It's time to summarize everything in your own personal discovery inventory. You might want to look back over Chapters 5 and 7 to be sure you haven't left out any interests or free-time pursuits.

To complete your inventory, make a list of your drivers, dreams, interests, accomplishments, strengths, and skills.

Personal Discovery Inventory
Drivers
Dreams
Interests
Accomplishments
Strengths
Skills

You'll return to your personal discovery inventory in Chapter 10. In the next chapter, we're going to challenge you to put on new, rewired glasses to see work in a different light.

Chapter 9
Rethinking the World of Work

I'm working on getting my Master's in social work. Now that's work.

—Maggie, 59, *retired PR exec*

If you think you know all about work, think again! In Chapter 1, we turned retirement on its head. In this chapter, we turn work on its head. Throughout this book we've challenged you to look at yourself in an expanded way. Now we challenge you to look at work in an expanded way.

Most people view work through too rigid a filter, usually in terms of their pre-retirement job or career. As recruiters, we've seen how this narrow definition of work leaves out areas with the potential for fulfillment. We don't want you to miss anything, so we show you how to think more broadly about work, in the following four categories: *work for wages, work for fee, work for me,* and *work for free.* These are four distinct categories, but they aren't mutually exclusive. In other words, if you're painting a mural, that could be work for fee and work for me. How you categorize work also depends on a person's perspective. For example, starting a business could be work for fee or work for me, depending on your perspective. Looking at work this way is like looking through a wide-angle lens. Seeing the big picture or the new vista of work enables you to better see potential rewired work opportunities.

Beyond *having* to work, our research showed that people *want* to work because they want to remain productive and vital. The happiest rewirees do not look at work one-dimensionally—whether you raise prize-winning roses, run marathons, or prepare tax returns seasonally, work is involved. In this chapter, we show how the four categories of work, either in combination or individually, can be the foundation of a fulfilling rewired life. You may already be involved in one, two, or even three of the categories but haven't thought about how to put them together in a balanced work portfolio. This chapter shows real people doing this successfully. Some of these people admitted to us that they never thought they would find these combinations of work as exciting or challenging as their pre-retirement work. But they did.

Work for Wages

Work for wages means working as an employee and getting a W-2. This might include working for either for-profit or non-profit corporations, working for small businesses, or working part-time. When people think about work in the traditional sense, working for wages is usually what comes to mind.

Real People: Evelyn

Evelyn retired from the military in her early 50s as a high-ranking officer. She hoped to get a leadership position in an organization that served either young girls' or women's needs. She joined a major nonprofit organization that focused on young girls' development. Her management skills transferred well, and the new position fulfilled her visibility and structure drivers.

Tip

Categories are in the eye of the beholder. Volunteering might be work for me for one person and work for free for another.

Real People: Leo

Leo, whose family had run restaurants, retired at 65 from a Fortune 100 company and went into the restaurant business in New Jersey, paying himself as an employee. Leo had been an accountant all his life, and he liked it well enough, but found it was never social enough for him. When he announced his plans to go into the restaurant business, his family and friends were shocked. They had assumed he would either retire completely and play golf or continue working as an accountant forever, winding down into a solo accounting practice. Instead, Leo said he felt working in the restaurant business was what he should have done all along.

Being both financially savvy and practical, Leo thought about buying a franchise, but instead bought a restaurant someone was "retiring" from. He has built it up into a profitable and sociable place. Leo recently decided to create a new concept and put in a deli next door to his restaurant. Both are doing well, and he couldn't be happier in his rewired career. In going from work for wages at a major corporation to work for wages in a completely different business, Leo has gone into a business where he is highly motivated and fulfilled.

Tip

Remember, your skills are portable. With today's globalization, your skills might be even more valuable in foreign markets.

Work for Fee

Work for fee refers to work where you are paid a fee and receive a 1099 tax form instead of a W-2. It can be as steady as a full-time job, or it can be far more sporadic, depending on your desires and the demand for your services. You can get a fee for almost any conceivable service rendered, from information to knowledge, to practical things, such as graphic design, dog walking, furniture finishing, or catering.

Work for fee may include doing what you did for a living working for wages, or it can be something altogether different, but the key to working for fee is knowing someone who will buy your services. Work for a fee allows you flexibility, and you work on your own terms.

Real People: Ellen

Ellen, now 63, retired at age 50 with a two-year phased retirement plan. A happily married woman with no children, Ellen spent her entire career at one telecommunications company, working her way up to higher positions at a time when women were not necessarily in the running. Two of Ellen's top drivers were accomplishments and recognition.

At age 50, she was offered the chance to do a special project in Europe that would allow her to phase into retirement instead of being downsized. She jumped at the chance. She discovered, much to her surprise, that she liked project consulting. Moreover, her telecommunications skills were in demand in Europe.

After the two-year phased assignment, she returned to the United States and started a consulting practice. Her husband was supportive and flexible because he owned his own business. For the next 10 years Ellen consulted, until many of her clients retired. After that, she just let her consulting practice lapse and focused on working for free.

Phasing Into Retirement

Here are some pointers on phased situations compiled from *HR Magazine:*

Make the case for retaining you instead of replacing you. It's often much cheaper for companies to keep employees than to retrain them.

A common employment situation for retirees is part-time, 20 to 30 hours a week. Does your employer offer this option? Does it offer health benefits for part-timers?

If you are drawing pension benefits, your only choice might be to return as a nonemployee outside contractor to avoid the legal problems with pension benefits being paid to workers who are employees. Investigate all the options at your company.

Inquire about the maximum number of hours the company will allow you to work and still retain pension and medical benefits.

Phased retirements are currently most common in higher education and government. Use examples from these fields as models if the concept is new to your employer.

Ask for a pilot program to test the concept if your employer has never tried it.

Ask to make phased retirement available by job category, not by person. This might make it easier for your employer to avoid landing afoul of discrimination issues.

If your employer isn't open to phased retirements, ask about part-time work, consulting, or paid three-month leaves of absence to try out retirement.[1]

2001 HR Magazine. Adapted with the permission of HR Magazine, published by the Society for Human Resource Management (www.shrm.org), Alexandria, VA.

Real People: Harry

In Harry's version of rewiring, he went from working for wages to working for fee, back to working for wages, ending up working for a former competitor. Harry, 61, retired after 35 years with a large, successful aerospace manufacturer in California. The company offered him and several hundred other employees an early retirement package that was too good to pass up. He had been a senior technical director, and he loved what he did. His wife, Bev, had her own career as a mid-level manager in a bank and planned to work several more years.

Harry knew he wanted to continue to be involved in the technical side of aerospace on a part-time basis. He received a job offer that enabled him to work two or three days a week for a consulting fee. Additionally, he was paid to write articles for a professional journal. Harry kept up his professional image, and the part-time income was a great supplement to his retirement income.

One day, the president of a former competitor called and invited Harry to lunch. At lunch, the president told Harry that he was making some organizational changes and would like Harry to come to work for him. This time, Harry could write his own job description and build his own department. The compensation was generous. After four years in retirement, Harry went back to work.

Real People: Laura

Laura returned to a lifelong passion, fiction writing, as her rewired career. She had been in big-city law enforcement and had a high position and a high media profile. At 54, she decided to retire from the force to pursue novel writing as her full-time rewired career. Writing was a lifelong love that she had pursued in college. After college, when she realized she couldn't support herself writing fiction, she pursued law, her second love. Several years ago, to test the waters, she returned to novel writing and successfully published her first book. Making the most of everything she had, Laura even used her work environment and the city locale as backdrops for her fiction. Many people have dreams about writing, but Laura actually did it.

Real People: Sam

Sam, 59, is a retired math teacher. He and his wife love music, and one of their first trips after retiring was to the Spoleto Music Festival in Charleston, South Carolina. Although Sam loved being able to spend several days at the festival, the experience made him realize that he was being too passive about his passion for music—he felt he was on the outside looking in.

One day he was talking to a group of his wife's friends who were asking him questions about a composer. He cavalierly said, "Come over at 10 A.M. on Saturday, and I'll introduce you to Johann Sebastian Bach!"

This off-the-cuff comment led to Sam's turning a hobby, music, into a retirement career. He began to give impromptu classes at home. Eventually, young mothers asked Sam if he would teach a paid class for little children, and he was asked by the local community college to teach a music appreciation class there. A budget-driven saver, Sam is thrilled about the extra money he makes from this "hobby" and the fact that he now feels he is valued.

Real People: Jane

Jane, 59, is a vivacious extrovert who attended the Yale Drama School and pursued improvisational theater early in life. After 15 years of waiting for her big break, she decided to get a "real job" and went into sales. She became extremely successful, and over a 12-year period grew into managerial positions at her company. At 52, she was tired of worrying about sales quotas and training new executives. At a high school reunion, she met a former classmate who had retired from practicing law and had gone into mediation. Jane realized that she, too, had what it takes to be a good mediator: problem-solving skills, strong verbal and listening skills, and the ability to think on her feet.

Jane began to investigate what it would take to become a mediator while still in her sales job. She found mediation seminars and classes within driving distance and attended them on weekends and during vacation. Mediation will be a good rewired career for Jane because it's portable and flexible. She and her husband are thinking about retiring to their summer community, and she can be a mediator there. And the flexibility allows her to cut back on her schedule later if she wants to. When the day comes, she imagines doing some traveling with her husband first and then returning to begin her new retirement career as a mediator.

Work for Me

The third category of work is *work for me*. This is any type of work you do for yourself, for your own pleasure. It can be paid or not. It could include working on your bridge game, working at your golf game, working on a Master's degree, working on the Great American Novel, getting a private pilot's license, or learning to cook Thai food.

Real People: Terry

Terry, 60, who had been in regional banking all of her work life, got caught in her company's latest round of downsizings. She was offered "education money," which allowed her to take a class of her choice that could lead to future employment or enjoyment.

Originally from Belgium, Terry's family had been involved in the chocolate business and bestowed the treasured recipes on her. For fun, she took a chocolate-making class and fell in love with the art and adventure of making delectable chocolates. She started selectively making chocolates for family members and friends and for special occasions only. People were thrilled with the chocolates and by the genuine pleasure Terry got from being a chocolatier.

A local restaurateur asked if she would supply him a limited amount of chocolates weekly. When he wanted to increase his order with her, she balked at first, not wanting to turn her passion into a full-blown business. But then she proposed producing moderate quantities, once a week, excluding the months of April through September, and he accepted. Terry loves what she's doing, and she's never felt more in control.

Real People: Pete

Pete, 68, had been in the hotel business for more than 40 years. He had worked for many companies during his career, but no matter where he had to move his family, he always planted a garden. To Pete, flowers made wherever they were living a real home. When Pete retired, his goal was to raise glorious flowers as his own personal joy.

Receiving Pete's full attention, the garden became a show-place. It was selected for the garden tour by a local organization and was profiled in a specialty magazine. Pete was pleased but realized that he had already developed his garden beyond his wildest dreams. He was looking for something else. When his neighbor, the local florist, asked if he would ever consider help-ing out at the store during the holidays, Pete said, "Why not?"

Pete's "helping out" at the florist's shop started at Christmas and then led to Valentine's Day and then Easter. Pete decided to study flower arranging and is now considering doing free-lance flower arranging. The florist had tried to convince Pete to become a partner in the business, but Pete wanted to work on his schedule and not be beholden to a time clock again.

What You Can Afford

As you begin to imagine opportunities in the four categories of work, you have to know what you can afford. Because finances impact what type of work you select, before you make any life changes, ask yourself the following questions:

➡ Do I have to keep working to pay the rent/mortgage?

➡ Do I want to work to supplement a pension or 401(k)?

➡ Do I simply want "pin money" for an extra golf game at the municipal course?

➡ Am I going to work to fulfill drivers and not worry about money?

➡ Do I think that if I'm going to work, it had better be for big money, regardless of whether I need it or not?

➡ Do I need to get paid for any work because that's the only way I'll value the work and my participation?

How you answer these questions will affect the opportunities you select for your rewired work portfolio in Chapter 11.

Work for Free

Work for free is volunteer work broadly interpreted. It includes working for any number of traditional volunteer organizations such as the Red Cross and Big Brothers/Big Sisters, helping out elderly or underprivileged people in your community, or simply giving a helping hand to someone in need. If you volunteer as a trail leader at a state park, or drive for Meals on Wheels, or sit on the board of your public library, that's work for free.

Work for free also includes work done for the benefit of others that isn't part of any formal organization. For example, if you organize a one-time dinner for the benefit of a family in need in your community, or organize a tribute to an outstanding community volunteer, that's work for free.

Our research showed that work for free is a very important part of retirees' satisfaction, and many pre-retirees anticipate it will be for them, too. When it comes to working for free, the bottom line is to be sure that you really care about the issue and the organization and are comfortable with the people. No matter what the issue is, there's likely an organization or website that supports it, but you have to have the interest. At the end of the day, people feel fulfilled because they feel they are working toward a goal they really believe in.

The person who wants to give out the food in the soup kitchen is not going to be happy sitting for two hours at a board meeting, and vice versa. Here are some other considerations:

How much time, energy, and monetary commitment do you want to make? For example, when it comes to doing hands-on work, do you want it to be weekly, daily, or monthly? How much responsibility do you want to undertake?

Many people look to work for free as their chance to make a difference or leave a legacy. As you think about your work choices, you might also ask yourself, *Do I have a specific mission I was put on Earth to fulfill? Will any of these opportunities lead me there?*

When you think of work for free, think broadly. Nonprofits run the gamut from A to Z. If you're not sure where to start, ask yourself if you're interested in any of these issues: children, civic or community issues, disease prevention, disaster assistance, drug abuse prevention, education, international issues, and local or national politics.

Tip

Most people think only of local and regional organizations when they think of work for free, but you shouldn't overlook state, national, and international organizations as well.

If you don't find an organization ready-made in your area of interest, you might think about starting one. That's what the retired volunteer physicians did who founded the Samaritan House clinic in San Mateo, California. This free clinic for the poor is staffed by retired physician volunteers, with only a salaried medical director and administrator. Because the clinic does not have to deal with managed care, the physicians are able to practice medicine the way they think it should be practiced. They have the time to develop real human contact between themselves and their patients, a precious payoff for the free services. "Sometimes I think we should be paying the clients for what we get out of this," said Dr. Marks, a physician on staff.

Real People: Martha

Martha, 68, a Ph.D. in New York City, left academia and went into the corporate world, where she specialized in training and development. With her strength in career development coaching, she eventually opened a highly successful practice.

On her sixty-eighth birthday, she closed her practice to focus on her health and fun. After September 11, Martha wanted to help the number of people who had lost their jobs. She got in touch with an organization helping the unemployed job seekers by giving them advice on resumé development and networking strategies. Martha began volunteering there, working with groups of people in weekly sessions.

Many of the people she counseled wanted to see her privately, but Martha chose not to reopen her practice. Some friends were surprised to see Martha giving away her time and thought she was selling herself short by giving away her expertise. Martha says she is doing what she loves, on her terms, and she has the freedom to take on private clients later if she changes her mind.

The New Realities of Work

The stories and examples in this chapter reflect important trends in the world of work.

Working in a Third Way

Although the phrase "working retirement" used to be an oxymoron, it no longer is. The new employment trend is that people receive retirement benefits and continue to stay in the paid labor force in some form, blending two formerly exclusive categories. We've given you lots of examples in this book of people who have rewired and are "working in a third way," our term for this new employment trend. People are starting to see retirement as the technical age at which you can qualify to collect retirement benefits, and nothing more than that.

Real Quotes
I wanna bop 'til I drop.
—Ted, 60

Mobility

Another new reality is that people are moving easily from one category of work to another. The mobility offered by the four categories of work is one of its most powerful benefits. You can control your movement among categories as your interests, needs, and circumstances change. As some of the stories in this chapter illustrate, you can also stop work and still restart it later.

Diversified Portfolios

A final reality of the new world of work is that the term *diversified portfolio* relates as much to your work life as to your financial life! Your financial planner talks about diversification in terms of stocks, bonds, and other investment vehicles. Just as you don't want your portfolio all in one investment, you might not want to have just one kind of work in your work portfolio.

You have the opportunity to get the most out of your work portfolio by choosing from among the four categories of work. The combinations are endless! You just have to be open to new thinking.

Real Quotes

For a full life, aging and working are tied together .... When work isn't allowing growth that's satisfying, we begin to feel and act old.
—Helen Harkness, Ph.D.[2]

Donna, one of our Real People, is an example of the diversified work portfolio in action. Her work portfolio encompasses a fulfilling combination of three work categories: work for me, work for wages, and work for free.

Real People: Donna

Donna had had a very successful corporate career. At 53, she lost her position as CEO of a communications company when it was sold. She left with a good financial package and lots of free time. Donna told us when we interviewed her for this book that she had always been self-directed and knew her hot buttons.

She had no intention of winding down. She had a list of ideas she couldn't wait to put into play. The first was to get herself fit and healthy (work for me). Donna was teaching a college-level public relations course, a position she had tried out a few years earlier (work for wages) and loved. Always known as a giver of both time and money, she also sat on several nonprofit boards (work for free).

A search firm contacted her six months after she retired, regarding a full-time position as executive director of a high-profile women's disease foundation (work for wages). She was excited by the opportunity and, after accepting, put her teaching on hold and resigned from one board. Most recently, she agreed to serve as president of a prestigious women's organization (work for free).

It's Your Turn

As the examples of rewired work in this chapter have demonstrated, the potential combinations of work you can do in *rewirement* are limited only by your imagination. The next chapter shows you how to put your imagination to work to discover your own rewired possibilities.

Chapter 10
Imagine the Possibilities

When I listed all of my accomplishments, I realized I still wanted more of them!

—*Bill, 69, retired retailer*

In this chapter, the findings from your inner and outer explorations come together. As we've said, the premise of rewiring is to know what you'll be leaving behind and to know how you'll replace it in the future. In this chapter, you begin to identify the replacements, which we call *possibilities*.

Up to now, you've completed a series of exercises that have forced you to answer some tough, personal questions. You've delved into yourself, created your personal discovery inventory, and seen the expanded world of work. You're armed with a lot of self-knowledge, and to quote one of the pre-retirees we interviewed, you're "ready to take the act on the road." The question is, which road offers the greatest fulfillment?

This chapter completes step four of the *rewire* process. In this chapter, you create your *rewirement* possibilities menu, a list of work possibilities you might pursue. Three steps are involved:

1. *Brainstorming* to create your list of possibilities.
2. *Evaluating* to screen your possibilities against your drivers, the rest of your personal discovery inventory, your calendar analyses, audience, other considerations, and your own intuition.

3. *Prioritizing* to rank your *rewirement* possibilities menu according to how well each of the possibilities matches your drivers, the rest of your personal discovery inventory, and other considerations. After you've ranked the whole list, you will focus on your top five. You will use your top five possibilities in Chapter 11.

Brainstorming Possibilities

The ideal way for us to help you come up with work possibilities would be for us to sit down and brainstorm with you. That's obviously impossible, so we've decided to do the next best thing: illustrate the process using our sessions with the four pre-retirees. We believe that sharing their interviews will help you see how you can come up with possibilities when you brainstorm on your own (the evaluating and prioritizing steps of the four pre-retirees are not shown).

First, however, here are a few general pointers that came out of our personal brainstorming sessions with the pre-retirees:

Start with the obvious. The first things to brainstorm about are the area or areas in your life that you feel strongest about, even if it's something about which you have little knowledge. We started our brainstorming sessions with the pre-retirees' strongest interests in their professional and personal lives. You should do the same.

Generate lots of possibilities, and don't worry whether they're practical. Your goal in brainstorming possibilities is to let out the kite. Imagine every possible idea, no matter how crazy. Try to come up with as many possibilities as you can, and don't worry about whether they are too far out. You can always pull the kite back in when you evaluate the possibilities in step 2. You want the richest ideas possible.

" Real Quotes

I think it's a good idea to think big and age little.
—Rev. William Sloane Coffin[1]   "

Imagine using your skills in a different context. One technique that's useful is to select a skill you already have and imagine how it can be applied in a completely different context—for example, a different field or type of organization. Your skills are transferable; where else could you take them?

Use brainstorming to generate more questions. When we met with the four pre-retirees, they were each in very different stages of their rewired thinking. The clearer an idea you have about what you want to do, the easier it is to come up with possibilities. When you don't have a clear idea, you need to ask yourself lots of questions to clarify your thinking. You may need to do more thinking and possibly more research.

Take your time. You'll probably need to sit down and brainstorm more than once. You might want to leave a few days between sessions. Write down *everything*. We advocate a healthy, open mind-set as you come up with possibilities. Check your cynicism at the door.

Identifying Work Categories

When you see the pre-retirees' lists of possibilities, you'll notice that one of the four work categories described in Chapter 9 has been listed next to each. Work categories can be used for brainstorming. Let's say you're an art director. You could come up with possibilities in each category, as in the following table.

Art Director

Wages	Fee	Me	Free
Ad agency	Consulting	Paint for self	Teach kids art
Retail stores	Design projects	Learn new techniques	Art therapy
Magazine illustrator	Paint murals in nursing homes	View art	Do portraits of people
Teach art classes	Jacket/book design	Take art appreciation class	Donate artwork for specific causes

Tip

Don't penalize yourself by maintaining too rigid a definition of success, or you might deny yourself some terrific possibilities.

We now present the brainstorming of our four pre-retirees—Tom, Paula, Bob, and Carol—allowing you to see their outcomes before you do it yourself. Due to space constraints, we had to trim their lists, so don't use these shorter lists as a model. Think of as many possibilities as you can.

Pre-Retiree: Tom

Tom surprised us by saying that he had changed his mind and didn't want to retire in six months after all, although he will leave his company. Although he was excited about rewiring, he now realized that his original dream of golf, golf, and more golf wouldn't be challenging enough for him. He also had taken a lesson from the volatility of the stock market and knew he didn't want to have to worry about not having an income.

Sales positions. As Tom worked through the exercises, he realized sales was his life, but he needed to rethink how he could be involved in sales in a less pressurized way. He brainstormed these ideas:

➡ Promote a regional sales manager to his job and take his place with less management pressure.

➡ Do sales training and development for his current company.

➡ Sell for a competitor if he dared or wanted to, and if it didn't conflict with his noncompete clause.

➡ Sell a totally unrelated product.

➡ Provide sales consulting on technology needs to small and midsize businesses.

Sales and golf. We wondered if there was a way Tom could combine two of his strongest interests, golf and selling. Tom came up with these ideas:

➡ Sell a line of golf clubs or related products or apparel.

➡ Sell a line of any type of sporting goods.

➡ Buy a logo machine and sell monogrammed golf shirts, towels, and so on, to golf clubs direct.

➡ Get involved with investors/realtors in the sale of golf properties.

➡ Join a sports marketing organization.

Entrepreneurial. Tom has always had entrepreneurial ideas in the back of his mind, but he's never pursued them. In our brainstorming, Tom was on a roll and decided that he might …

➡ Start his own sales training/customer service firm.

➡ Create a consortium of trainers.

➡ Create a coaching and sales effectiveness company that specializes in salespeople.

➡ Open up a sporting goods store or franchise.

➡ Write a book on sales success and schedule speaking events.

➡ Create a sales course for lawyers and accountants.

Acting. Tom says with a smile that one of the reasons he's a good salesperson is that he's a good actor. He was proud of his prior acting accomplishments. People have always told him he has a great voice, and he wondered what he could do with it. He brainstormed these possibilities relating to acting:

➡ Get a voice coach.

➡ Take acting lessons.

➡ Go on a nonequity audition.

➡ Develop a stand-up sales training comedy routine.

➡ Model himself after John Cleese and create sales training videos.

➡ Do voice-overs for products that need a strong sales pitch.

Tom ended his brainstorming session with a few ideas that were solely joy-of-golf related, including playing golf on America's top 100 courses, going to the Masters in Augusta, Georgia, and teaching golf at the local high school. He noted that these could lead to business or new possibilities. Tom presents his top five in Chapter 11.

Pre-Retiree: Paula

Paula wants to pull back but not retire completely. She told us she knew she needed visibility and thought her lack of it in her prior two retirements was one reason why they hadn't worked out. With Paula, we started with her most immediate need—her business. Until she could determine how and what to do with it, she couldn't figure out what to do with the rest of her life.

Identifying business possibilities. Paula was interested first and foremost in unloading some of the responsibilities in her human resources business. Here's the list of possibilities:

➡ Sell her business to one of her associates and stay on part-time.

➡ Sell her business to a competitor and secure a three-year contract.

➡ Sell the business to one of her associates and take on a rainmaker role only.

➡ Keep the company but either promote someone from within or bring in someone from outside to handle the day-to-day management.

➡ Take a partner who will buy the company in the near future.

➡ Create a strategic alliance with a competitive firm and take a turnover fee.

➡ Do a roll-up of her firm with other firms and have one of their presidents take over.

➡ Take only a few select clients and work from home.

➡ Work with venture capital groups whose companies need HR consulting.

➡ Delete big consulting initiatives from the company offering.

➡ Close the business and go to work for a competitor.

HR-related ideas that also emerged include these:

➡ Do freelance writing for HR newsletters and publications.

➡ Write a book on HR issues or on family businesses.

➡ Give paid global HR seminars.

➡ Create paid keynote address speeches on HR topics and get on a speaker's bureau.

➡ Become an adjunct professor.

Sailing and HR. We then looked at Paula's passion, sailing, and wondered if there were ways to combine sailing and HR. Here's the list:

➡ Investigate whether any manufacturers of sailing equipment or related paraphernalia need HR consulting work.

➡ Get a client to sponsor a sailing trip for its clients for promotional or marketing purposes.

➡ Check out which CEOs/presidents are sailors and might be potential clients.

➡ Offer HR consulting services to sailing-related nonprofits.

➡ Write an article in *Sailing* magazine about how passions can lead to business; hope to get some business from it.

➡ Write a book that combines HR tools and sailing.

➡ Develop a paid HR team-building course for corporations, "Sail Your Way to Successful Staffing."

Real Quotes

Coming up with possibilities is like twisting a towel. To get the most ideas, you have to keep wringing the towel tighter and tighter.
—Marc Myers, author of *How to Make Luck Happen*

Sailing and young girls. Next, we looked at whether we could tie sailing to her interest in developing young girls' self-esteem:

➡ Charter a boat and test-market a skills-building, confidence-increasing class for foster children or inner-city kids.

➡ Charter or buy a boat and give free sailing lessons to needy girls.

➡ Get a national or local company that sells to girls to sponsor a self-esteem sailing course.

➡ Teach a sailing class through the local YWCA, Girl Scouts, or Girls, Inc.

➡ Work with the city's foster children department on a sailing trip.

➡ Have the national HR association create a mentoring program for foster kids or inner-city kids.

➡ Create a client-driven, cause-related corporate marketing initiative around kids and sailing.

➡ Mentor one child herself.

Foster care. Because Paula grew up in foster care, this was a subject dear to her, too:

➡ Contribute to the next mayoral race and begin to build relationships with city hall to help foster children by advocating for foster children.

Paula ended up with four lists of possibilities in areas she cares about—in business, sailing and HR, sailing and young girls, and foster care. We'll see Paula's top five in Chapter 11.

Pre-Retiree: Bob

Bob wants a phased situation at his company, but he hasn't spoken to his management yet. Because the phased situation had never been done in Bob's department, we focused on that first when we sat down with him. We asked Bob the following questions about the phased situation.

Phased situation. The first area we focused on was his idea of a phased situation at work.

➡ Why does he want a phased plan?

➡ Does he dislike engineering?

➡ Does he want out of his job function?

➡ Does he want to test the idea of retirement?

➡ Does he want to find another opportunity at the company or elsewhere?

➡ Has he tackled the phased concept from a feasibility standpoint, including management and colleagues' reactions?

➡ Does he know what he wants from the phased situation (salary, benefits, hours, duration, management responsibility, interaction with colleagues, etc.)?

➡ Has he talked to HR about any phased roles within the total corporation and how they worked out?

➡ Has he checked outside of the company to get ideas on how to make the phased situation work best?

➡ Has he determined how/when is the best time to speak to the boss about the idea—a meeting or a meal?

Community interests at the company. Bob wanted to investigate working in community initiatives and other nonprofit situations at the company (whether phased or not). For many years, Bob had spearheaded the community outreach activities at his company, and he had headed the United Way initiative. Here are the ideas Bob came up with:

➡ Move to the company's charitable giving department.

➡ Move into the community affairs department.

➡ Become a two-year, on-loan executive to a nonprofit with salary paid for by his corporation.

➡ Set up scholarships/internships and co-op opportunities with engineering students and the company.

➡ Work with marketing to create strategic alliances or promotional events with community organizations.

➡ Set up website opportunities and contests for future engineering students.

Giving back. Bob could take his community mind-set directly outside and into the nonprofit arena. Here's the list Bob came up with:

➡ Run a nonprofit as an executive director.

➡ Become a nonprofit executive recruiter.

➡ Join or start a nonprofit strategic consulting or development firm.

➡ Deliver paid speeches and seminars on nonprofit board governance.

➡ Work for a charitable foundation.

➡ Become a development officer.

Church. Bob is a lay leader in his local Episcopalian church, and for years he has wondered if he has a calling into the ministry. Bob brainstormed these possibilities:

➡ Pursue the ministry.

➡ Do paid fund-raising for the national church, in the States and globally.

➡ Do missionary work, in the States or globally.

➡ Write spiritual novels.

➡ Get involved with the organizations building Episcopalian retirement communities.

➡ Develop a course to show churches how to successfully use corporate tools in a church environment.

Personal interests. Bob's World War I interest was a natural to brainstorm against:

➡ Write and speak on favorite aspects of WWI.

➡ Set up a website and chat site for WWI memorabilia collectors.

➡ Join or create WWI tours in France.

➡ Delve through WWI archives in London and France as a paid researcher.

➡ Caretake a WWI cemetery or monument in Europe.

➡ Write a novel with a WWI theme.

We'll see Bob's top five possibilities in Chapter 11.

Pre-Retiree: Carol

We discovered that Carol had a vision with no details. Her brainstorming consisted of creative questioning of possibilities.

What do you see yourself doing? We began by asking Carol what she actually saw herself doing for or with animals. When she couldn't come up with any concrete ideas, we asked her general questions to try to flesh out her interests:

➡ Hands on or not?

➡ Sitting at a desk directing others?

➡ Literally rescuing animals?

➡ Getting animals in shelters adopted?

➡ Starting or building a shelter or adoption center?

➡ Donating her own money or fund-raising?

➡ Giving only time?

➡ Working alone or with other organizations?

➡ Saving specific breeds of animals?

➡ Saving endangered species (globally or in the United States)?

➡ Offering scholarships to vet students who would commit to working with abused animals?

➡ Training animals for hospital work?

Combining care for animals with other interests. Next, we asked Carol to consider how she might combine other strong interests in her life—politics and art—with her love of animals. Here's the list of questions she considered:

➡ Advocacy/lobbying on spaying and neutering issues or on animal welfare?

➡ Fund-raising for animal-related groups only?

➡ Creating a coalition of animal foundation presidents and executive directors to meet with politicians?

➡ Promoting artists who do animal paintings as fund-raising ideas? Calendars? Stationery?

➡ Tie-ins with national consumer products companies that have pet food divisions?

➡ Creating a catalogue of pet and pet-owner gift items as a fund-raiser?

When Carol saw the abundance of possibilities, she knew that she would have to do some more focusing on her own. She realized that she needed to do more research. We return to Carol in Chapter 11.

Coming Up with Your Own Possibilities

Now that you've seen the pre-retirees go through the brainstorming process, it's time for you to do the same. Hopefully, you've seen the power and importance of this step.

Step 1: Brainstorming

Think back over what you've learned about yourself. Through the *rewire* process so far, you have discovered your drivers, created your personal discovery inventory, and completed the analysis of your intellectual/physical side through the calendar analysis and strengths/skills review. Think also about any concerns or intentions you may have at this point that you may not have taken into account. Use everything you know about yourself and then proceed on gut-feeling or instinct.

Think about the topics you'd like to brainstorm. Have fun and be creative. This process works in both up and down job markets because it's a tool to help you prioritize what's important to you.

Possibility Potholes

Being too linear in your thinking.

Being too rational.

Using money as the criterion/measurement for everything.

Saying, "Unless I can make a big, visible difference, I won't do it."

Thinking too small.

Saying "I could never do that."

Not seeing beyond or getting out of the present.

Being risk-averse.

Psychological inertia.

Possibilities take time to make happen, some longer than others, so it's never too soon to start brainstorming. If even a kernel of an idea exists, jot it down. Don't discard anything at this point—you'll do that later. A possibility doesn't have to gel or even make sense at this point. And remember to use your imagination.

If you're really stumped, ask others for ideas. They may have ideas or possibilities you like. Write down any possibility you or they think of. Nothing is off-limits for the creation of your next act!

Tip

Use tools that make brainstorming easier for you. Stick Post-it notes on the wall, use an easel, write in a journal, or carry colored index cards with a different color for each idea. You might even talk into a tape recorder or use your cell phone's voice notes feature.

Step 2: Evaluating

The next step is to screen your *rewirement* possibilities menu against your drivers and the rest of the items in your personal discovery inventory. How many of the possibilities match your drivers and your dreams, interests, accomplishments, strengths, and skills? On this second pass, take into account your intuition or gut instinct, as well as your calendar analyses and audience considerations, discarding those that don't feel right and you wouldn't consider pursuing. What possibilities screen well and feel right? Add a possibility you haven't considered previously if it pops into your mind.

Step 3: Prioritizing

Next, go through your list and rank your possibilities. You can rank all of them or just cherry pick your top five possibilities. Write down your top five. For your own reference, jot down your rationale—why you are choosing one over another—for your ranking. Give yourself ample time to choose. In the next chapter, you start to act on your possibilities.

Step V
Putting Your Action Plan in Motion

Chapter 11
Possibilities in Action

I thought the stress of work would kill me; now I'm afraid the boredom of retirement will.

—Ken, 63, doctor

In Chapter 1, we said the first step in the *rewire* process is "to recognize that rewiring is a going *to.*" You are now at the point of deciding where you're going and are ready to develop the action plan to get you there. In this chapter, you select your #1 possibility, create a profile of the important issues relating to that possibility, and write an action plan to make it happen.

Possibility Profile

A possibility profile is like a job description used in the executive search process. For corporate searches, the client states what they're looking for in an employee. In your case, it's the other way around: you're in the driver's seat, and you're noting what you're looking for in terms of possible rewired work situations and why. The possibility profile is a helpful tool because it gets people to spell out in black and white what they're looking for in their customized rewired positions.

Before creating your own possibility profile, let's return to the four pre-retirees: Tom, Paula, Bob, and Carol. They've just come back from completing their evaluations of the possibilities they identified in Chapter 10. They honed their lists to their top five possibilities, and they are focused. More insights resulted in some changes in their plans.

Pre-Retiree: Tom

Tom told us he decided to stick to his plan of taking retirement from his company in six months, but without the steady diet of golf, golf, and more golf. Tom admits that although he sees the big picture, he had been nearsighted about himself. He had thought his choice was an either/or, but now he sees it isn't. He thought he wanted to leave sales entirely, but now he sees he just wants to switch to a different kind of sales. Tom told us he was a little surprised by what he chose as his top five possibilities. Here they are, along with the reasons why he chose them:

#1 Join a golf equipment or golf-related manufacturer in a sales capacity. Tom says he's a salesman and always will be. He likes making deals. He realizes he was frustrated with his job and that's why he wanted to leave sales altogether. As he says, "I love the chase, but not all the pressure." He wants to sell something golf-related, perhaps golf equipment, or work as a golf manufacturer's rep. He brings personal passion, as well as local connections, to this kind of sales.

#2 Become a professional voice-over actor. Thinking over his lifetime of accomplishments, Tom rediscovered something he once had fun with, but had long forgotten about: he had found theatrical productions a gas in high school and college. Sure, it was a long time ago, he admitted, but people continued to tell him that he had a great voice. Why not pursue voice-overs and see if there was something there? He could take some acting lessons, get an agent, go on casting calls, and go to New York's Broadway shows more frequently. Even if he doesn't find acting work, the acting classes would sharpen his presentation skills.

#3 Start a sales training/customer service company. Tom likes the idea of starting his own sales training/customer service company. Over the years, he has trained salespeople who went on to very successful positions. Tom feels his training initiatives are unique, and he hasn't been very impressed with the sales training companies out there. He'd like to run his own shop.

#4 Produce and distribute a teaching/etiquette golf video for kids. Tom has noticed the growth trend in kids' golf and how their parents support it. He thinks he could produce and market a kids' golf video, which he would market to parents. He is also thinking of developing it into an online teaching concept. The golf etiquette concept could also be extended to adults who are new to golf, and perhaps even to seniors.

#5 Work for a sports marketing organization. Another angle Tom is interested in is selling sponsorships for sporting events. Tom thinks it could be interesting to be in sales with a company that sells sponsorships—he knows someone who did that for the 2002 Winter Olympics. Tom knows his sales skills are right on, but he doesn't know if his years in technology would be seen as valuable or not. Also, he wonders if his overall years in sales will be a positive or a negative.

The next step for Tom is to write his possibility profile. Tom wrote profiles for all five of his possibilities, but due to space, we only show the profile for his first choice. Tom's possibility profile is in the following box.

Tom's Possibility Profile

Possibility: Join a golf equipment or golf-related manufacturer in a sales capacity.

Drivers fulfilled: Competitive, goals, social, structure.

Desired outcome: Sales position with a company that has a great product line and potential.

Desired audience: People involved in the golf industry, including clients, associations, pro shops, golf clubs, resorts that attract golfers, and organizations that help children get involved in golf.

Work category: Work for wages/work for fee.

Money considerations: Salary or commission plus bonus, in addition to Tom's investment portfolio.

continues

continued

Time commitment: Full-time and some weekends, not more than 15 percent travel.

Physical considerations: None (Tom's in excellent physical shape).

Strengths used:

Balanced

Confident

Direct

Friendly

Looks the part

Sense of humor

Thorough/well prepared

Skills used:

Acting

Athletic

Closing

Interpersonal

Making it/luck happen

Presenting

Selling/persuading

Socializing

Downsides:

Doesn't know the people in the industry.

Doesn't know the industry (learning curve).

Ways to overcome downsides:

Convince employer that his passion for golf will carry him.

It's easier for a salesperson to go from technology to golf than the other way around.

Future work implications:

Tom has been avidly involved in golf in his free time. Deepening his contacts in the professional side of golf might lead to further opportunities.

Meet new people who live, breathe, and eat golf.

Family implications: Tom's wife is already a golf widow and is willing to take up golf.

Profile objective: Investigate move from technology sales to golf-related sales.

Tom is now ready to develop the action plan, or steps to take, to make the possibility profile happen. Here's his action plan, in logical order.

Tom's Action Plan

1. Talk to the pro at his club to find out more about the golf equipment industry.

2. Identify what level of sales position his ego would allow him to pursue.

3. Ask the club pro to set up discreet networking meetings with a couple of the club's suppliers so Tom can get an overview of that side of the business.

4. Visit all the golf shops and sporting goods stores in his area. Ask the retailers which manufacturers are perceived as cutting edge, and which are doing poorly.

5. Attend golf industry trade shows and conventions to find out more about the products and companies involved.

6. Look at the classified ads in the golf magazines to see what the companies are looking for.

7. Ask club pro to set up a game with some golf vendors who he thinks might be receptive to Tom's goal.

Pre-Retiree: Paula

Paula admitted to us that she was a "serial retiree"—and tired of it. Because her two previous retirements had failed, Paula wanted to get it right this time. When we started brainstorming, she was hung up on the idea of leaving the day-to-day contact with her 10 employees because that would leave a blank space in her life. When Paula came back from evaluating her possibilities, she said she never realized she had such a rich list of options and choices that she valued and believed in. She could see that her life had a purpose, and she was ready to move on.

#1 Take a partner into the business. Finding a partner is Paula's #1 possibility because it will provide her an exit strategy from her business. The right partner will free up her time, provide cash, enable her to do things with more visibility (a driver of paramount importance to Paula), and allow her to still have her name on the door. Deep down, she knows that by sacrificing some control in her business, she will extend her working life and have a better quality of life overall. She will know that what she has created won't disappear.

#2 Charter a boat and test-market a skills-building, confidence-increasing class for foster children or inner-city kids. Paula had a long list of sailing possibilities and was interested in them all, but finally chose the one about foster children because she had been a foster child herself. Giving time is more meaningful to Paula than just writing checks, and she likes to be a role model for kids. Paula, who is trained as a sailing instructor, is especially interested in teaching team sailing as a way to boost the kids' self-esteem. She has a bigger vision for the team sailing concept but wants to test-market it before she brings in clients and sponsorships.

#3 Check out which CEOs or presidents are sailors and might be potential clients. Paula would like to find clients who are not only sailors but also decision-makers. Such people may become a new audience for Paula and may provide invaluable support for possibility #2.

#4 Contribute to the next mayoral race and begin to build relationships with City Hall. Paula knows that local and state issues impact negatively on foster care. She is thinking that the best way to improve lives for foster kids might be from the inside out. Getting involved with politics and the decision-makers could one day lead her to a position to enact change as a political appointee.

#5 Develop a team-building sailing seminar to sell to her clients. Paula feels that if she is putting time into crafting a seminar for the foster children, maybe she could adapt it for off-site seminars for corporations. If the team sailing concept works for foster kids, it might work in business, too. This could lead to a seafaring seminar consulting company!

The next step for Paula is to write her possibility profile. (As with all pre-retirees, only the first possibility is shown.)

Paula's Possibility Profile

Possibility: Take on a business partner who will enhance the business service offering and eventually give her an exit strategy.

Drivers fulfilled: Intellectual stimulation, problem-solving, value, visibility.

Desired outcomes: Reduced day-to-day management responsibilities and the time to focus on select clients.

Desired audience: Current clients, industry associations, media and business groups.

Work category: Work for wages.

Money consideration: Salary plus Social Security, pension, and retirement savings.

continues

continued

Time commitment: Fridays off and complete buy-out in three years.

Physical considerations: Paula's annual physical confirmed that overall she is in good health, but she has high cholesterol. Her physician has suggested that she spend more time exercising and incorporate stress reduction in her daily regimen.

Strengths used:

Cause-driven

Entrepreneurial

Inspirational

Maintains a presence

Skills used:

Marketing/self-marketing

Presenting

Problem-solving

Transporting (sailing)

Vision/envisioning

Downsides:

Loss of control in her business when a partner comes in.

Turning over of employees and clients to the partner.

Ways to overcome downsides:

Learn new management style by hiring a management coach.

Embrace improved quality of life.

Future work implications: Paula will use her authority as an HR consultant to open other kinds of doors that may lead to more support for sailing initiatives relating to foster kids.

Family implications: More time to spend with her daughter. Paula hopes a few clients will continue as friends after her business relationship with them ends.

Profile objective: To begin a major shift in her business life to free up her time.

The last step for Paula is to create her action plan to achieve the profile objective, to begin a major shift in her business life to free up her time. Here is Paula's plan.

Paula's Action Plan

1. Define how she sees herself in a new business setup.

2. Prepare a list of what she wants (including qualifications) in a partner.

3. Meet with her lawyer, accountant, and business associates to determine what it will mean legally and financially to her to bring in a partner, and see if they have any recommendations.

4. Develop a clear understanding of the various partnership elements that could make the position attractive to someone.

5. Draw up a list of candidates (consultants, competitors, clients) who would be potential partners.

6. Take a trusted client into her confidence to see if they have a recommendation.

7. Prepare a list of networking resources she can talk to for leads on candidates.

8. Talk to an executive coach about her management style. Paula knows her strengths. She also knows that her weaknesses might lead to complications with a partner, and she wants to deal with that soon because the process takes time.

9. Set a reasonable time expectation.

10. Meet possible candidates.

11. Determine how to maintain confidentiality until she is ready to tell employees.

Pre-Retiree: Bob

Bob started by saying that it has become clear to him that he doesn't want a phased situation. He doesn't want to look like he's "checking out." He recognized that he wants to stay involved with new challenges. While sitting in a task force meeting on implementing the new technology at his company's manufacturing plants, he saw that there may be a possibility of being in charge of implementing the new technology, and he'd like to pursue that as his #1 possibility. There are several different ways he could go with his new possibility, and he will have to evaluate his options. After thinking about all of our questions, he said, he discovered that he wants a very different set of responsibilities. His wife was right—she had been telling him all along to do something different, that he wasn't his old self. He just hadn't been sure which direction to go in.

#1 Identify the best role to implement the new technology. Bob is on a task force to review the purchase of a very costly new type of technology for his company's manufacturing plants. He is intrigued with the new technology. It hasn't been decided who will be responsible for overseeing the implementation of the system on the company side. He wants to explore three options: being put in charge of implementation at the company, taking retirement from his company and joining the technology supplier as an employee working on the project, or retiring and working with the technology supplier as an independent contractor on the project. If he learns the technology in-depth, that could lead to owning his own consulting business specializing in this new technology, which could lead to global opportunities.

#2 Investigate the ministry. Bob would like to investigate the ministry in a broader way. He knows seminary would require three years to complete and ordination is a lengthy and selective process with no guarantees. Bob is a leader in his local Episcopal church in Detroit, where he has served for many years as warden.

His spiritual side deepened after September 11, when he assisted the ministers in setting up and running special counseling sessions for the congregation. He saw how people responded to his caring and confident style.

Tip
An outside event can inspire your rewired thinking and direction. Keep an open mind.

#3 Run a nonprofit as executive director and *#4 Join/start a development/fund-raising consulting firm.* Bob groups possibilities #3 and #4 because they both relate to an important driver, to make a difference. He has been leading his company's community outreach programs for a long time, and Bob recognizes that his experiences and connections could lead to the nonprofit world. But he doesn't think he's ready to make that professional move yet. He has a strong sense that he can make this move in the future if he stays involved with his current nonprofits and keeps up his presence with key people and issues. He knows he could give and get a lot by being a leader in the not-for-profit world.

#5 Manage a World War I cemetery in France. Bob, a World War I aficionado, has dreamt of caretaking a WWI cemetery in France ever since his first visit there. He never thought what it would actually be like until he looked at the possibility in terms of his drivers. It scored low, fulfilling only lifelong learning, and leaving his recognition and being an authority drivers unfulfilled. Even worse, being in France, his belonging driver would totally be out of the picture. Bob doesn't want to walk away from his dream, so he's going to pursue how he can "pull it out" to make it more driver-fulfilling (do it as a vacation, do it once as a unique volunteer opportunity, etc.). He is going to do this simultaneously as he pursues his top two possibilities.

The next step for Bob is to write his possibility profile.

Bob's Possibility Profile

Possibility: Identify the best role to implement the new technology.

Drivers fulfilled: Authority, belonging, lifelong learning, recognition.

Desired outcome: Learn new technology that could lead to global consulting opportunities.

Desired audience: All levels at both the corporation and the supplier, from plant managers to the highest levels of management.

Work category: Work for wages or work for fee.

Money consideration: Bob, the company, and the supplier all have to evaluate what will be the most advantageous to them from a financial, tax, and legal standpoint.

Time commitment: Full-time, at least three years. Foreign travel approximately 30 percent.

Physical considerations: Bad sinuses could be affected by additional air travel.

Strengths used:

Confident

Goal-driven

Good values

Honest

Smart

Takes responsibility

Trustworthy

Skills used:

Consensus-building

Decision-making

Managing

Prioritizing

Problem-solving

Teaching/instructing

Team-/alliance-building

Technical skills

Values diversity

Downsides:

Relinquish his charitable outreach responsibilities at corporate.

This will not be his project—he will be implementing a taskforce project that continues to involve many decision-makers.

Ways to overcome downsides:

Bob may have to relinquish his outreach responsibilities at corporate, but his new focus on church activities might offset that.

Bob's trustworthiness will go a long way with the staff implementing the technology.

Future work implications: Implementing the new technology will give him highly marketable skills that could lead to global consulting assignments in the future, as well as a close relationship with the supplier. He could become a roving troubleshooter in engineering facilities worldwide.

Family implications: Foreign travel is new, but maybe his wife, a retired teacher, could join him.

Profile objective: To start the investigation process.

Now that Bob has identified his profile objective to start the investigation process, he is ready to develop the action plan to support it.

Bob's Action Plan

1. Review task-force notes to see how the new technology implementation project is being planned.

2. Assess all aspects of the implementation to spot hidden problems and make sure he feels comfortable with current plan.

3. Script out why he's the right guy to implement the new technology and the three different ways he could do it: working for the company, working for the supplier, or working as an independent consultant.

4. Evaluate the contacts and network that will support him in his desire to get the new position.

5. Determine if he has any competition for the position.

6. Create a succession plan for his department, including time-tables, but don't make it public until he secures the other position.

7. Present his proposal to the key decision-maker(s).

8. Drum up support and endorsements.

9. Talk to other people within the company who have moved from a business unit to a consulting-type role.

10. Separately make a list of the potential upsides and downsides of the position and discuss them with his wife.

Pre-Retiree: Carol

Carol had left the brainstorming session with tons of questions, but once she stepped back, she realized that she was 90 percent sure she wanted to create a state-of-the-art adoption facility for homeless animals in her region. Carol is initially going to fund the project herself, so she first wants to be sure what she pursues is really needed by the animal community. Carol said she got emotionally caught up in the need to help animals before she researched what was missing from animal services in the local community.

Carol will pursue her #1 possibility: to create a new 501(3) organization whose mission it is to enhance the lives of homeless animals.

The next step is for Carol to write her possibility profile.

Carol's Possibility Profile

Possibility: Build a new type of adoption facility for homeless animals in her local area.

Drivers fulfilled: Action, exposure to people, fulfillment, have an identity, make a difference.

Desired outcomes: To find out the greatest needs and challenges in saving or placing homeless animals, with a primary focus on dogs, if that's possible. Her dream is to create an organization whose mission is to help dogs get into healthy living situations.

Desired audience: Movers and shakers in the animal, political, and business communities.

Work category: Work for free and then maybe for wages.

Money consideration: Carol is funding the project and has appropriated seed money. She would eventually do major fund-raising and grant writing.

Time commitment: Whatever it takes.

Physical considerations: She has the enthusiasm and the stamina to do the necessary research.

Strengths used:

Ambitious

Charismatic

Connector of people

Enthusiastic

Financially astute

Focused

Passionate

continues

---

continued

Self-motivated

Smart

Strategic

Skills used:

Analytical

Asking (fund-raising)

Building

Financial managing

Leadership

Planning

Thinking/outside-the-box thinking

Downsides: Carol will have supporters and detractors. The animal rights people may be territorial and may not share information if they think Carol is going to intrude on their turf.

Ways to overcome downsides: Carol will have a good idea ahead of time who her allies and enemies will be and will assess how to deal with her strongest opponents.

Future work implications:

Position as founder/executive director of the organization, once it's established.

Consultant to other groups.

Work for a manufacturer of animal products.

Family implications: Carol's husband, a retired journalist, hopes she doesn't get so caught up in her new project that it encroaches on their travel schedule.

Profile objective: To research the national, state, and local issues on homeless animals.

Carol wrote down the action plan for her profile objective, to research the national, state, and local issues on homeless animals.

Carol's Action Plan

1. Determine who could help her identify a model organization, the current activists, potential allies and foes, foundations that give money to animal rights issues, and local business leaders who are supportive of animal rights issues.

2. Identify the major issues facing animal rights organizations, including the national ASPCA and Humane Society.

3. Identify animal rights organizations that could be potential strategic alliance partners.

4. See what white papers have been written on key issues.

5. Construct an interview checklist of issues and opportunities.

6. Interview the local activists in her community to see what their issues are and to get names of other individuals to interview.

7. Do a physical but "discreet" interview at all of the tri-state and local animal shelters.

8. Connect with leadership of Maddie's Place, a role model adoption center in San Francisco, and Best Friends Animal Sanctuary in Utah, to get questions answered and relationships built.

9. Ask key people to sit on an advisory council as the concept develops.

10. Develop a business plan model to be completed after the research.

As you can see, the four pre-retirees have chosen four completely different possibilities, which will take them in four completely different directions when they *rewire*. But the beauty of it is that they are able to organize and make their very different rewired plans happen because they are all using their possibility profile and the action plan.

It's Your Turn

Now it's your turn to write your own possibility profile. From the list of top five possibilities you created in Chapter 10, pick your #1 choice. You can pursue as many possibilities and write as many possibility profiles as you can manage, but for now, focus only on your top choice.

Choosing your top possibility doesn't lock you in for life, nor does it mean you have to do it after you investigate it. You can always come up with new possibilities in rewiring. Because we are living longer, it's possible to have many rewirings in a lifetime! Using possibility profiles and action plans, you can turn your possibilities into reality as many times as you like. There's no end to rewiring.

Your Possibility Profile

The possibility profile is a way for you to double-check that your possibility will deliver what you want it to. Remember the real people from Chapter 1 who flunked retirement? Maybe they wouldn't have if they had used the possibility profile. If you find that any of the criteria in the possibility profile aren't what you're looking for, you may need to revisit the possibility.

Here's a reminder about what the possibility profile should contain:

Possibility: Write a description of the work you want, as concisely as possible.

Drivers fulfilled: List your drivers fulfilled by the possibility.

Desired outcome: What you hope to get from the possibility.

Desired audience: Audiences you will interact with.

Work category: For wages, for fee, for me, or for free.

Money considerations: Financial impact.

Time commitment: Time involved (hours a week, etc.), travel.

Physical considerations: Physical considerations such as health and mobility.

Strengths used: Strengths you'll use.

Skills used: Skills you'll use.

Downsides: Trade-offs or things you may have to give up.

Future work implications: Future work benefits that may evolve from this.

Family implications: Impact on family.

Profile objective: What you need to do first.

Your Action Plan

Now that you've written your possibility profile, the next step is to write your action plan. The action plan consists of the steps you'll take to make your possibility a reality. We know we can't hold your hand here, but if you need ideas, review the four pre-retirees' action plans in this chapter and see if any of their ideas can apply to your situation. Write your action plan now.

Having finished this chapter, written your possibility profile and an action plan for it, you have all the tools you need to *rewire*, except the most important tool of all: the right perspective. Without the right overall approach, your *rewire* journey won't be as successful as it could be.

Chapter 12
Perspectives and Realities

I wish we had had the guts to talk about the future before we retired. We could have saved ourselves some grief and had a lot more fun.

—*Joan, 64, rewired retiree*

Now we'll shift gears in the rewiring process to recognize a key reality—you don't *rewire* in a vacuum. In our research, we discovered that people were naïve when it came to understanding how particular outside realities could disrupt their plans for the future, as well as how their pursuits would impact others. Three key realities—relationship, societal, and workplace—can significantly affect how you approach and accomplish your rewiring. This chapter addresses all three.

Note that some of the realities will be more relevant to you than others, depending on your personal situation and possibility profiles. Use the realities to test your thinking about the future. Consider how your expectations align with those of your family, society, and workplace.

Relationship Realities

The first realities we consider are relationship realities, specifically couples. We are constantly asked, "How do you *rewire* as a couple?" It doesn't matter if a couple is retiring together, if one is at home already, if one partner is 10 years from being retirement-eligible or from selling a business, or if one partner never plans to retire. Relationship implications exist for each situation that will impact the pursuit of your rewired dreams.

Does your thinking include anyone else who will be affected? Who else cares about your rewiring? Who else needs to be a part of your planning? They should be included in your plans. That's why family considerations are included on the possibility profile. Take a minute to reflect on what you wrote about your possibility profile in Chapter 10.

Let's Talk

Couples told us that they had to chart and navigate a new course when they became empty-nesters. It's the same with rewiring. It's about defining his, her, and our needs for the future. The challenge is to not make any assumptions about what your partner is thinking. Create a dialogue. You might not initially be on the same page about the future, but that doesn't mean you can't get there. We discovered that many couples have difficulty communicating with each other and that talking about their hopes, fears, and dreams was difficult. Other couples admit that starting the conversation was challenging but was worth it just to find out what their partner was thinking. They reported that conversation helped them better understand the situation and their individual expectations.

We'll use a variety of Real People stories to illustrate the relationship realities. Our research shows that sharing other people's stories helps people see pitfalls and opportunities within their own relationships.

Real People: Carl

Carl, 60, a recently retired chemical engineer, was surprised to learn that his wife had many possibilities that didn't include him. He said he was hurt at first and wondered if his marriage was in trouble. He viewed his wife as his social director and realized she didn't want the job. After two months of puttering around the basement and garage—and trying to make his wife feel guilty—Carl realized that his wife had given him the freedom to become the musician he had always dreamed of becoming. Now, Carl feels a little vulnerable and has accepted that he might never become a great musician, but he'll have fun trying. His biggest surprise was that he had assumed his wife would create his fun for him.

How to Begin the Couples Dialogue

One of the partners has to take the role of initiator. The initiator should think about what, where, and how to begin the discussion. The initiator needs to be thoughtful about when and where to start the conversation and select an environment the partner likes. Select a time to talk when you'll have few distractions, listen as much as you speak, and be prepared to compromise.

Real People: Bob and Toni

Bob, 62, is a partner in a technology consulting firm he'd started nine years earlier. His wife, Toni, 59, is a retired computer consultant. On a dare from a friend, they worked through the rewiring process and discovered that Bob had identified only one possibility: he wanted to cut back to working only four days a week. Toni, who had six possibilities, was upset to see that Bob was not ready to sell the business and *rewire*. She accepted that his work gave him great driver fulfillment but asked that he think about an eventual exit strategy with a time frame. Bob said he felt that Toni finally understood how important business success was to him.

Caution for Couples

Your challenges as a rewiring couple include money management, health, fitness, sex, communication, social engagement, and family. Below the surface are questions about how to use your two most precious resources: time and money. Go slow and be patient with one another.

In our couples seminars, we overheard wives telling their husbands, "You can't follow me around the house all day." "Don't ask me what I'm going to do." "Go out and get your own life between 9 and 5." The messages might sound hurtful at first, but this doesn't mean the wives don't love their husbands. They are simply saying, "We need a plan for you, me, and us."

Real People: Elizabeth and Al

Elizabeth was in one of our seminars and introduced herself as the wife of a recovering flunked retiree. She thought she and Al would travel in retirement, but instead, she said she watched her energetic, social husband retire to a reclusive life of watching TV and reading the paper. She described herself as growing sad, frustrated, and angry until she realized that Al had lost his purpose. He had always complained about the number of e-mails he got at work, and now he was complaining that he never got any! After two years in retirement, Al rewired and went back to work part-time for a former supplier. Elizabeth says they now take long weekend trips to accommodate Al's new work schedule. She admits the travel isn't what she imagined, but she views it as temporary, and Al's new purpose totally worth it.

Tip

When couples say they will be living "separate lives" in the future, it doesn't mean they're separating, but rather pursuing activities that are important to them as individuals, rather than as a couple.

Couples and Money

Managing money in retirement can be a challenge, especially as we live longer. One of your possibilities might be to pursue a new career. Your action plan might call for you going back to school for a degree, new training, or a certification. This could lead to a discussion with your partner about using your money to invest in yourself. Be prepared to show how spending the money and the time on the pursuit of new work will positively impact both of your futures.

Real People: Bernice and Cal

Bernice, now 72, initially retired at 64 from an accounting firm. After 23 months, she decided that golf and sitting on a corporate board were not giving her enough driver fulfillment. She was a leader without a cause or a challenge. Her psychologist daughter realized she was getting depressed and suggested she find a new purpose. She was thrilled to become the executive director of a nationally prominent nonprofit.

Her husband, Cal, however, wanted to travel and spend time living abroad. Every time he raised the subject, Bernice had an excuse: too busy in her new role, too expensive right now, we will do it when I really retire. Cal became frustrated but started to travel with his golfing buddies or alone. "Now," Cal says, "I'm 74 and Bernice is finally ready to pack. I've already done my trips. I wish we had communicated better early on. We could have blocked out a few months after Bernice retired and tried living abroad."

In each of these situations, partners need to have realistic expectations of the other. Assuming your spouse will change is not a good *rewirement* strategy.

Family Considerations

Many retirees have elderly parents or grandchildren who may require their time and attention. Planning for these responsibilities should be factored into your *rewirement* plan.

Tip

Adult children can view your retirement as a benefit to them—free baby-sitting! If caring for grandchildren appeals to you, great, but do it on your schedule. Don't feel guilty if you're not always around. You're rewiring and that's keeping you happy and healthy—and they'll benefit from that!

Couples and Sex

Many husbands and wives believe that creating a rewired life with less stress can be a tonic to a renewed sex life. But it doesn't always happen. Viagra has altered couples' expectations about sex. As one man put it, "Now Grandpa wants to play with Grandma, but she only wants to play with the grandchildren."

On the flip side, without rewiring and finding new purpose, many individuals can fall into a funk and experience a loss of self-esteem, which can lead to depression and a decline in everything, including sex. If you or someone you know is having difficulty, suggest they speak to a physician or therapist.

Societal Realities

Now we look at social realities, one of the biggest of which is ageism. Like it or not, we live in a youth-obsessed society.

The Two-Headed Monster

Ageism exists both in society and in our own heads. And both have to be dealt with if you are to succeed in your rewiring. As research has shown, older workers are more expensive (because seniority tends to lead to larger salaries) and are disproportionately let go in economic downturns, despite legal protections.[1]

Real Quotes

Age discrimination in employment is unlawful. Individuals 40 years old and older are protected from age-related discrimination by the Age Discrimination in Employment Act (ADEA). It prohibits employers from using age as a factor in making employment decisions about workers. All aspects of employment are included from hiring, training, and promotion opportunities, to termination. Companies may not advertise for young workers or mandate a particular retirement age. Employers, however, may expect all workers, regardless of age, to perform adequately in their roles. Older workers should remember that the ADEA does not protect them from job actions because of unsatisfactory performance.

—Deborah Weinstein, Esq., The Weinstein Firm

Cracks in the Silver Ceiling

Although society won't change its negative impressions about aging overnight, we are beginning to see real cracks in the "silver ceiling," the point at which age becomes a serious obstacle to employment. There are still stories in the press about it, but they're declining. In fact, some companies are retaining their mature workers and others are recruiting older employees into new organizations because some younger workers don't have the necessary skills required for the job—something mature workers might have. The shift to age appreciation will be gradual and will probably depend on how drastic the skills shortage actually is.

There's widespread controversy about what's the best approach to dealing with society's negative attitudes about age, and we found that opinions varied. Some people recommend avoiding direct confrontation about age. Others seek legal redress. Many people report that age has never been a problem for them.

Are You Ageist?

Through our research, we have seen many people inadvertently playing into society's negative image of aging. A 90-year-old woman we met takes the blood pressure of senior citizens because she "likes to take care of old people." She saw all seniors, except herself, as old. We have come to conclude that we are all ageists to some degree and shouldn't be. Don't play into it by using any of the negative words about age—at any age!

Focus on Functional Age, Not Chronological Age

Age is a great excuse. Listen carefully when people start to say things like "I can't do that. I'm too old." As noted career counselor Helen Harkness says, "Without realizing it, our chronological age can unconsciously and automatically block our thinking about our future."[2] It's important to not let yourself get caught in this negative trap. If you begin to see your age itself as limiting, it will be, and the limiting attitudes may keep you from achieving the life of your dreams. If you're in this position, evaluate the role negative thinking is playing in your plans.

Rewirees who are more focused on their functional age are more successful when they *rewire* because they don't let their age limit their choices. Successful rewirees never give up pursuing their goals and dreams, no matter what their age. They don't go around believing that they're too old to do what they want. Instead of believing negative age stereotypes, successful rewirees believe it's never too late to chase a dream.

Workplace Realities

Now for a big-picture overview of workplace trends. For specifics on handling workplace issues when you *rewire,* see Chapter 13.

Labor Shortages

Although the Bureau of Labor Statistics says there will be a labor shortage of 10 million workers by 2010, not everyone agrees. More importantly for rewirees is that there's no guarantee that an ultimate shortage will be in your industry or in your skill set. Research conducted by The Conference Board, Merrill Lynch, AARP, and others indicates that organizations are at all points on the spectrum in recognizing and preparing for this anticipated shortage. If "working in retirement" is one of your selected possibilities, you need to know what organizations are doing or not doing.

On the good news front, the U.S. Equal Employment Opportunity Commission (EEOC) recently announced a proposal to amend the ADEA (Age Discrimination in Employment Act), which "... would permit employers to favor older individuals because of age."

Many industries are already experiencing skills shortages and have special programs in place to recruit and retain experienced workers. The industries include aerospace, defense, health care, nursing, oil, gas, energy, transportation, and retail. (See Appendix B for specific resources.)

New Work Titles and Options

Low unemployment, competitive wages, and employee requests have compelled organizations to consider work options that offer increased flexibility. We listed several options in Chapter 2, including flex-time, freelancers, contract workers, consultants, and part-time. Additional work options include independent contractors, project workers, free agents, project managers, seasonal workers, flexible workers, and temp and interim workers.

For example, as an independent contractor, you might be able to work as a consultant paid a fee. If you qualify under IRS rules, you become a self-employed independent contractor. This works well for very short-term assignments. And CVS, The Home Depot, and other companies have created *seasonal worker* programs that permit you to work where you want, when you want. If you live in Maine in the summer and are a snowbird in the winter, these companies allow you to do the same job in different states. If you need flexibility, investigate who else might be offering seasonal jobs.

Tip

Check out the List of AARP Best Employers for Workers Over 50 at www.aarp.org/money/careers/employerresourcecenter/ bestemployers.

Phased Retirement

There's no standard definition for phased retirement. A pre-retiree told us he'd like to phase or "downshift." Many organizations are testing phased retirement models that are legally compliant and meet employer and employee needs. The government is seeking to enact legislation that would permit flexibility within the federal government that could affect the private sector as well. Look into what your organization, vendors, and customers are doing. You may get some new ideas.

The Rehired Retiree

Your former employer(s) or the company you retired from may rehire you. Companies have historically done a poor job at knowledge transfer, so when employees retire, they take their job knowledge and expertise with them, leaving behind an information gap. To close this gap, companies are rehiring retirees who know the company, the job, the equipment, the people, the informal communications network, and the shortcuts that save time and effort.

It used to be that if a retiree were brought back full-time, the individual would have to suspend collecting his or her pension. But a new type of employer called the *third-party employer* permits the collection of your pension and a paycheck at the same time as you work full-time. One such company—and a fast-growing one at that—is ZeroChaos in Orlando, Florida. Here's how it works: you become an employee of the third-party company and then work on-site at your former company. The third party payrolls you, in many cases offering benefits, including health care and a 401(k). The third-party employer remits the payroll taxes to the proper authorities and provides human resource support to assist with any issues that arise.

New Role of Staffing Companies

Adecco, Kelly, Manpower, and Spherion are major staffing companies that supply workers to a wide clientele. Today, staffing companies supply a whole range of unskilled and skilled workers, including lawyers, accountants, graphic designers, engineers, etc.—the list of jobs offered is as vast and varied as the clientele. Staffing companies are also becoming more creative in how they access and support their workers, including retirees.

Smaller staffing firms are recruiting mature workers, too. They usually focus on specific job categories, such as lawyers, accountants, information technology professionals, etc.

Some offer free training programs that can lead to job certifications, and flexible schedules may be a possibility. You might even be able to try out a new job as a temp and see if you like it. Go to the websites of the major staffing companies, and see if they are actively seeking to have mature workers and retirees register as part of their labor pool (see Appendix B).

Online Work Opportunities

People of all ages complain that they've applied for jobs online and never heard from anyone. The reality is people are getting hired, whether through company websites or sites like Monster.com, Execunet.com, Hotjobs.com, Careerbuilder.com, retirementjobs.com, or retiredbrains.com. Opportunities in the not-for-profit sector can be found on idealist.org and volunteer-match.org. See Appendix B for others.

You can use these websites for many purposes:

➡ Search out jobs that fill one of your possibilities.

➡ Get information—salary data, educational opportunities, career advice, etc.

➡ Read articles to get ideas about jobs and trends—whether you want full-time or project work or are a consultant looking to get ideas.

➡ Search for job description keywords and include them on your resumé.

But note: websites should not be your only source of information.

Tip

Your resumé should be computer search friendly, which means having keywords or phrases that best describe your skills. This is helpful when your resumé is scanned by a computer program. It increases the chance of your resumé being selected.

Advice for the 50+ Entrepreneur

The federal government estimates almost 3 million business own-ers are over the age of 55—an increase of almost one third since 2000.[3] For many, having their own business is a dream come true. For others, the dream can quickly turn into a nightmare. More than 50 percent of all new businesses fail in the first four years. "There's a myth that entrepreneurs have special traits that distinguish them from other people," says Raffi Amit, academic director of Wharton's Goergen Entrepreneurial Management Programs. "There's a myth that entrepreneurs are risk takers. But research has shown that they try to manage risk."

If you decide to go the entrepreneurial route, ask yourself a long list of questions, including these:

➡ How hard am I willing to work?

➡ Can I manage risk?

➡ How much am I willing to invest in time and money?

➡ Can I make a profit with this business?

➡ How can I get benefits for myself and my employees?

Many colleges and adult education programs offer courses on starting your own business.

❝❝ Real Quotes

Being self-employed means hard work, long hours, six-day work weeks, and limited vacation time. I started my own retail con-sulting business after I retired. I thought that my age and energy level might be a problem, so I decided to bring in a younger partner. He is helping balance the work load so I can still have a family life.

—Milton, age 63 ❞❞

Rise of the Social Entrepreneur

Some people *rewire* into the not-for-profit sector, which includes paid and volunteer work. Some of them become social entrepreneurs. According to Ashoka.org, "Social entrepreneurs are individuals with innovative solutions to society's most pressing problems." Social entrepreneurs start organizations to change for the better the way society functions.

Volunteering

Nonprofits are realizing that while individuals want to *rewire* to volunteer activities, they don't always have the financial flexibility required to work for free. Some organizations are subsidizing the cost of transportation and paying hourly wages.

Volunteer work is not what it used to be—here or abroad. Private and nonprofit organizations both are offering opportunities that combine service with vacation.

Tip

Become an intern or understudy at a business you're interested in to test the market and see if you really like the work involved.

Moving On

Before you venture out into the world, reflect on how the relationship, societal, and workplace realities discussed in this chapter might impact your possibilities and action plans. In the next chapter, we share myths and stereotypes about mature workers and offer specific suggestions and ideas that will positively affect how you present yourself as you move ahead into *rewirement.*

Chapter 13
Making It Happen

We are here to prove that Rocky Balboa isn't the only 60 year old looking for a challenge.[1]

—*Max Stier, president, The Partnership for Public Service*

We're nearing the end of the book, and you now have many of the tools you need to *rewire*. To give you a competitive edge, in this chapter, we offer some final insights and strategies you can adapt to any situation or possibility profile.

There's a reason futurists call our time right now the "Age of Individual Responsibility." Because it's all up to you. You're the one to make everything happen, whether you want to do work that's full-time, part-time, or seasonal; buy a franchise; open a boutique; join the Peace Corps; become a starter at a golf course; or do missionary work.

Mature Worker Myths

As you go forward, be aware that bosses, people who may hire you, and co-workers and colleagues will often have preconceived notions about mature workers that are wrong and based on myths and stereotypes.[2] Here are some negative myths about mature workers. Mature workers …

➡ Are set in their ways, slow to change, and can't be retrained.

➡ Don't know technology and are reluctant to learn.

➡ Have problems relating to younger workers or younger bosses.

➡ Are all planning on retiring as soon as they're retirement-eligible.

➡ Are not physically fit and have low energy.

➡ Think they have all the answers.

➡ Aren't staying current.

In the following sections, we show you ways to debunk these negative myths.

Mature Worker Realities

There are positives about the mature worker. The following widely acknowledged realities about mature workers also happen to be good reasons to hire you. Mature workers ...

➡ Are flexible and adaptable; change has been a constant.

➡ Have good time management skills.

➡ Can mentor others.

➡ Are reliable.

➡ Have the experience, insights, and knowledge that save time, reduce mistakes, and improve productivity.

➡ Understand workplace politics.

➡ Relate to older customers, clients, and suppliers.

➡ Are not necessarily seeking a promotion or a career path.

➡ Reduce employer turnover costs.

How you present yourself when you network and connect with others has a lot to do with how successful you will be in achieving your goals. The rest of this chapter includes ideas on how you can position yourself and leverage situations so others will want to help you "connect the dots."

Getting What You Want

Successful rewirees know that getting what you want depends on how you present yourself and your skills. It isn't just about what you do, but also about how you look. Time for a reality check!

Be Up-to-Date Skills-Wise

The biggest objection to older workers is that their skills are dated.[3] To deal with this, take courses, study, read, or get others to tutor you. Do whatever you have to do to be current in technology and communication skills. Be sure you have an e-mail account and know how to use it. If a new client or boss wants you to use a BlackBerry, be prepared to do so, or be prepared to turn down the assignment.

Be Up on the Lingo

Master the constantly changing language of the workplace, including new buzzwords, expressions, and phrases (e.g., *spaghetti marketing, blamestorming, upskilling,* etc.). Try to find out what the phrases mean before you meet potential clients or interview for paid or volunteer work, or even go on informational interviews. Look for new words and phrases when you read newspapers, magazines, or blogs, and search online to find out what they mean. Be up on what's new.[4]

Be Pro-*You*

You can further counteract age myths by offering strong and positive reasons why *you* can do the job. Eliminate any concerns up front. Tell interviewers why you're the person they should hire as a consultant, use as a volunteer, or put on a community board. Do your homework so you can link your strengths to the organization's profile.

Be Independent-Minded

The pre-retirees we've profiled throughout the book—Tom, Paula, Bob, Carol, and others—come from different backgrounds and have different *rewirement* goals. But they have one thing in common: they're all independent-minded enough to take control of their lives. They listen to what makes them tick. They don't wait around for "life" to happen; they go out and make it happen. One rewiree we worked with says that when someone says to him "You can't do that," his response is "Who says?"

Now that you've come this far in your *rewire* process, don't let anyone talk you out of it. You're aware of the relationship and societal realities that exist and are prepared to manage any challenges associated with them.

Be Adaptable

When they face situations that aren't perfect, rewirees aren't rigid. They don't define success too narrowly and don't need a single outcome to say a situation is a success. They are able to take in feedback, see alternatives, and adapt without giving up their dream. When they have to, they are also able to discard and move on.

Be Optimistic

Rewirees who get the most out of their rewired lives are optimistic, too. Even if you're not a natural optimist, try to practice optimism. Surround yourself with optimistic people, and stay away from negative people.

Tip

Do an attitude check. There is no replacement for a PMA—positive mental attitude. If you don't have one, work on developing one. Focus on attitude and effort, as these are the only two things in life we can control. And keep your sense of humor handy. When you laugh, your muscles relax, your breathing deepens, and oxygen fills your bloodstream. Laughing is good for the body, for the soul, and for those around you.

Be Unique

When you're in a grocery store, what do you see? Products of all types are sitting on shelves. What sets one apart from the others? How it looks? The message it conveys? Is it new and improved? Does it have greater efficacy?

What sets you apart? If you're looking to get a job or apply for a volunteer opportunity, what unique experience do you have that makes you different? What do you offer? Why should someone hire you? Suggest you run for office? Chair a committee?

Think about it a minute. How have you "packaged" yourself? Have you been "repackaged"? Should you be? Take another minute to think of how you are physically and mentally positioning yourself to friends and associates who could help you. Remember, you are the product. Make yourself unique.

Be Vital

Are you fit and healthy? If you are, it shows. Your energy is up and you've probably got a bounce in your step! Doors will open if you are seen as a vital, fit, positive person who cares and is passionate about what he or she is going after, as people are willing to help those who put out positive energy. Being passionate about an interest is an impression you want to convey. You do this through your energy, attitude, and sincerity.

One man we know, who is in his 60s, mentioned in an interview a recent climbing trip he took in Nepal. We're not saying you have to climb in the Himalayas, but be sure you're projecting an attitude that your age is not a hindrance to you trying and doing new and challenging things.

Tip

Adopt the motto WIT—whatever it takes. Show that you're willing to go the extra mile to get what you want. Present yourself as an energetic, enthusiastic, experienced individual who can get the job done!

It's important to keep your brain healthy and active, too. The Dana Alliance for Brain Initiatives and NRTA AARP's Education Community together have a program called "Staying Sharp," which to us sums it up. Check it out online at www.aarp.org/health/brain and www.dana.org/about/dabi.

Be Curious

We can't say enough about the importance of curiosity. Being curious stimulates the imagination, starts dialogue through questions, and sets you apart as someone who is really interested in the subject. When others think you're really interested in something, they'll become more engaged in your needs and try to be more helpful. Rewirees have admitted blowing networking opportunities because they didn't ask questions. They didn't want to be vulnerable so they walked away empty-handed. Dare to be like a kid—they always ask questions.

Be Current

We're not saying you have to get a whole new wardrobe or a face-lift, but don't look dated. Be sure you're not sporting clothing or hairstyles that make you look either too young or too old. The goal is to look "with it" and age-appropriate.

And don't assume a potential client has no dress code. Do a little investigation. Also, just because you "dress up" for meetings doesn't mean everyone does. As one rewiree said, "I walked into an industry luncheon and felt like a school principal. I was the only one with a tie!"

Be Relevant

A friend of ours in his 50s told us about a conversation he had while lunching with much younger colleagues. When the topic of Kennedy's death came up, everyone agreed how shocked they had been. They began to trade notes about where they were and how they heard:

"I remember it was around Thanksgiving," our friend said.

"No, it was in the summer," the woman responded.

"Oh, no! I'm sure it was in November. November 22. I remember it like it was yesterday."

"Oh you mean his father," she said, laughing. "We're talking about JFK Jr.!"

After our friend turned red in embarrassment, he realized his mistake. He had not considered the ages of his colleagues and their different viewpoints. They were from the baby bust generation (born 1965 through 1976) and the echo-boom generation (born 1977 through 1997). There's no way they had the presidential assassination of JFK Sr. as their frame of reference. They weren't even born yet.

It's important to be "with it" and know what the issues are outside your own generation. How in touch are you with what other generations think and feel? How often do you talk with people of different ages? Do you know what's going on today outside your peer group? To stay vital and plugged in, you should consider making friends with people of different ages.

Tip

Know what today's hot buttons are. Keep up with what's going on by following the newspapers and magazines. See the current movies so you know who's hot and, equally important, who's not. Watch award shows and read books on the best-seller lists.

Tell Your Story

Before you start exploring your possibilities, present your story in a resumé, bio, or CV or through a one-page, bullet-pointed, prioritized synopsis of your major accomplishments. (Use the format that best helps you and is appropriate for the role you're pursuing.) In a time-challenged world, this is a real help to the interviewer. Boiling your story down to a one-page accomplishment sheet helps people you're networking with better understand who you are, what you've done, and what makes you right for the role you're seeking.

Tip

Be sure you have a business card, too. It's better than having to write your name and number on a napkin or a piece of paper when someone asks for it.

No matter what, resumés should be no longer than two pages. Focus on your most recent, relevant experience and significant accomplishments. The last 10 work years should do it. If you have a unique set of credentials you earned earlier than the last 10 years, put them under a "Other Significant Experience" header.

The resumé rarely gets you the job, but it does set the stage for the conversation. Lack of a "story" or a poorly written resumé can disqualify you before you even get in the game. Many books and online tools are available to help you write your story.

Tip

Prepare a one-minute elevator speech of what you are looking to do. You might even create one for each possibility. But when discussing any work opportunities, don't give your age. Talk about early life or work experience only if it relates to the job you're discussing.

Network, Network, Network

Many believe that success is based on who you know, but we believe it is based on *who knows you*. Networking remains critical, regardless of your stage of life or type of possibility being pursued.

It's an essential process for getting information and getting results. As Barbra Streisand sang, "People need people." People are what networking is all about. Rewirees connect with people to explore and make their possibilities happen. They also use the information they get through their networking to rule out ideas, which saves time and money.

People don't network for the sake of networking. They do it when they need to learn things. If you dislike networking, do it gradually and in stages to make it more acceptable to you. Networking is all about a healthy give-and-take between people. If you have a need, ask somebody. If they have a need, they'll ask you. "Pure and simple, networking is all about relationships— keeping and cultivating them for life," says Andrea Nierenberg, a friend and president of The Nierenberg Group, a consulting firm in New York City.

Network Smart

Your networking activities should be both in-person and virtual, and could include meeting a person at Starbucks to get information as well as networking online. We recommend that you do an initial Internet word search on each of your possibilities. Gather information and lay a foundation for yourself. Doing your homework shows you went the extra mile and, more importantly, people expect it.

Tip

When networking, don't keep saying, "I know that," because you'll run the risk of being labeled a know-it-all. If that happens, your contact may never again network with you or refer you to others.

Social Networking

Powerful new ways of communicating have emerged on the web that allow people to expand their community and their knowledge. Look at social networking sites such as www. Linkedin.com as a new resource for connections and information. You can get caught up in the sites, though, so be sure to manage your time.

People who *rewire* network to ...

➡ Explore their possibilities.

➡ Discover and connect with the leaders or the key "people to know" in a specific area of interest.

➡ Ask key people what they think it will take to make a dream a reality. (*Hint:* Write down their comments. People are flattered when you do, and on the flip side, they hate it when you don't. At the very least, say you'll remember what they tell you.)

➡ Identify organizations, clubs, and associations to help gain knowledge of an interest, a cause, or a business.

➡ Stay up on new trends/products/technologies.

➡ Find out about costs/competition/job requirements.

➡ Know who the competition is for a specific opportunity.

➡ Find a mentor or role model.

➡ Stay relevant, cutting-edge, and in the game.

A good beginning is to identify who is in your network. Draw up a list of former and current work acquaintances, making a different list of people for each specific area of interest. Consider customers, co-workers, clients, lawyers, bankers, accountants, or anyone who you think could be helpful. Don't limit yourself by assuming someone can't help you. You never know! Include people of different ages, too. One rewiree was shocked to discover that all his business clients were in their late 50s and early 60s and all chose to sell their businesses within seven months of each other! It put him out of business. Think broadly. People with answers are all around you. You just have to know what to ask.

Tip

Today there are four generations in the workplace. Your networking should include someone from each generation.

Care and Feeding of Networks

If you already have a network, you'll want to strengthen and expand it. You need to feed and care for your network, and not just contact them when you need them. When was the last time you took someone to lunch or phoned someone in your network to share some useful information? Keep your network strong by reciprocating and letting people know you care. You won't *rewire* by yourself.

The Top Ten Networking Tips

1. You are going to network with people in person, via e-mail, and on message boards. You can even network in the movie line, on the ski slopes, in the wine store, and at the doctor's office.

2. Before you contact a person, script out what you want to say. You may be leaving your request on voicemail or sending it in an e-mail, so be concise.

3. When you connect with the person, offer a brief statement on what you're looking for. Be sure to expose your thinking so they can react to it and amplify it.

4. Say what you've learned so far from others and, if appropriate, whom you've spoken to already.

5. Ask their opinions, suggestions, and recommendations about other resources.

6. Listen.

7. Ask them who else you should speak to (try to get at least two names).

8. Be sensitive about taking up too much of their time in person, on the phone, or by the length of your e-mail.

continues

continued

The Top Ten Networking Tips

9. Wrap up the meeting by summarizing what they've said they would do for you and reiterate the next steps.

10. Write a thank-you note, including a brief summary of the follow-up. E-mail is okay.

Master the Informational Interview

Informational interviews are useful no matter what you're looking to do. You can use them to explore a dream, investigate an interest, seek out a volunteer position, gather information about specialized travel opportunities, or become an independent contractor. After your networking has gotten you the informational interview, here are some things to consider:

➡ Present what you want to do and why you're speaking to them. Be concise.

➡ Create a list of relevant questions to ask.

➡ Determine what skills and/or credentials are needed to achieve your goal and what's critical for success.

➡ Elicit possible obstacles or issues.

➡ Inquire about other resources and individuals to contact.

Tip

Align your skills and interests with employer needs. Use relevant examples of your experience to demonstrate that you are right for the position.

Use Your Fear Creatively

The people who seem to get the most out of *rewirement* acknowledge fear and use it creatively. "I have this theory that you should challenge your fears when you're in your sixties," says Jim, 65.[5]

Roger Rosenblatt, in his book *Rules for Aging*, refers to a useful fear technique as pushing the wheel forward.[6] He relates that jet pilots attempting to break the sound barrier instinctively pulled back on the wheel to slow the jet down after it neared the sound barrier and started to shake violently. When they did that, the planes inevitably crashed. The pilot who was first able to break the sound barrier pushed harder on the wheel.

The lesson: When you're facing fear, it's sometimes better to push harder when you feel like easing up.

Be Balanced

Other people rely on being balanced as a way to reduce tension. A big-picture perspective enables many to be positive and know that other opportunities would come along. Instead of seeing being an independent contractor as a ticket to instability, they're able to look at it as a free ticket to a customized schedule.

Be Creative

Sometimes rewiring means getting your creativity back after years of disuse. A woman we met from Charlotte, North Carolina, summed it up: "I'm excited about the future, but I don't know what I'll do. I've lost my creativity. I used to have an imagination, but first my parents, then guidance counselors, and finally corporate America beat it out of me. I would go to a marketing conference and hear a motivational speaker who told us to think out of the box. But when I tried to, my boss would tell me, 'Get back in the box—we were only kidding!' Now, I am committed to getting my creativity back!"

Living the best rewired life possible involves coming up with your own creative solutions. As you *rewire*, you'll make new connections, gain insight into yourself, and be challenged to think more broadly. You might even feel uncomfortable. Go with it. Let go of what we call "old think"—that certain way we perceive ourselves—and dare to create something new.

Don't Follow Someone Else's Dream

We discovered a new trend in our research. Retirement and *rewirement* are "going competitive." The stakes have been raised in the game we call "Can You Top My *Rewirement?*" How many great hobbies do you have? Which exotic places have you visited? What great boards do you sit on? What mountains have you climbed? We live in a competitive society where the most commonly asked question—"What do you do?"—has now crossed over into retirement and *rewirement.*

It's easy to get caught up in doing things to impress others. Don't fall into that trap, though. Don't plan your future on someone else's agenda. Stick to fulfilling your own drivers and dreams.

Never lose sight of what's important to you. Above all, be sure your *rewirement* is your own. The next time someone asks when was the last time you climbed Mt. Kilimanjaro, you can just say, "I don't find any driver fulfillment in that."

Your Rewired Journey

We created the concept of *rewirement* because we believe people should never stop growing and being productive. We have seen how meaningful work gives life purpose. But at the same time, we know that no one can force you to grow. For a rewired life to have meaning, the effort has to come from you.

We hope you'll take everything you've learned in this book and move forward to find the rewired life of your dreams. We wish you the most fulfilling rewired journey possible. Successful rewirees live by the motto: "If it is to be, it is up to me." Your tomorrow is in front of you. All you have to do is go for it.

Appendix A
The Ten Nuggets of Knowledge to Enhance Your Rewiring

Here's a summary of the feedback we've received from thousands of people across the country:

1. People who plan their finances often fail to plan their lifestyles. You need to plan your lifestyle the same way you plan your finances. If you think your retirement will *just evolve,* it probably will, but not necessarily into what you want. Ask yourself *What's next?* Start with the basic, jump-starter questions such as *What will I do with my time? Do I need a new routine? If I volunteer, will it be once a week or once a month? Will volunteering require a financial contribution, and did I build that into my financial plan?* No question is taboo.

2. Couples have unique challenges. It doesn't matter who is retiring; both partners are affected. But many couples don't know how to begin the personal dialogue. Couples often end up at cross-purposes—or at no purpose at all—because the dialogue never begins. Even couples who may start from the premise that they're "on the same page," often discover that communicating their needs is difficult. Three issues need to be considered: *What do* I *want? What do* you *want? What do* we *want?*

3. Retirement is about constant endings and new beginnings. Working, traveling, volunteering, exercising, and learning are just some of the activities that can be in your future, but maybe not all at the same time. You will go in and out of activities—some you can control and others you can't. Strenuous travel will end if health issues develop. Board positions will end because of an age limit of 70. Grandparents might miss seeing grandchildren if parents relocate. The future will be cyclical. Endings need to be managed and replaced with new sustaining and nourishing activities.

4. *Not everyone has a passion.* If you have a passion, congratulations! You're the envy of many. But we have discovered that most people are yearning to find a passion, and many are hoping it will jump out and grab them. It doesn't work that way. It's better to focus time, effort, energy, and/or money on an interest with the hope that it can turn into a passion. Don't wait for that one perfect passion.

5. *Find new purpose and meaning.* Work gives many people purpose and meaning. If you're one of these people, you'll need to find a new purpose. Ask the big questions. *Who am I? Who do I want to be? What will be my legacy?* Be patient with yourself. These answers do not come quickly.

6. *Working in retirement is good for you.* The saying "use it or lose it" applies to your brain, your body, and your skills. Major research studies show that doing work you enjoy and having purpose provide tremendous health benefits, reduce some forms of stress, and increase longevity. Being retrained for a new job or taking on new intellectual challenges can help keep you mentally sharp.

7. *Technology skills keep you in the game.* Be "up" on the latest technology, including (but not limited to) computers, cell phones, PDAs, e-mail, and the Internet. Being technology-enabled is one of the most important skills in today's world and opens the door to work opportunities, ease of communication, connection, and fun. People need to be technology-enabled, even if they're not working, so they can stay connected. Not being comfortable on e-mail is a major barrier to friendships and connections.

8. Online and offline communities are retirement lifelines. Being part of a community is key. There are many types of communities—geographic, spiritual, interest-based, as well as online social networking sites—where you can connect to others. Online communities are not a replacement for human contact, though. Balance virtual communities with real ones.

9. Beware of generational attitudes regarding work and retirement. When you dislike your job, regardless of your age, the fantasy of retirement looks appealing. Adult children often overlay their feelings about work on parents. Pre-retirees have told us their adult children are telling them that they "should" retire because they've worked hard, are "old," and have earned it. For example, a 37-year-old son who hates his job couldn't comprehend that his parents like their work and that work was where they felt valued. A daughter wanted her parents to sell their business because, as she said, "You have enough money." Her dad replied, "But we love what we do." Bravo!

10. Ageism is slowly eroding. Mature workers (defined by the Age Discrimination in Employment Act as anyone over the age of 40) are breaking the "silver ceiling" and shattering stereotypes and myths about aging. Don't fall into the ageist trap of thinking of yourself or others as being "too old" to try something new!

Appendix B
Online Resources for
REWIREMENT®

Websites change frequently, so you might want to do a keyword search for names similar to those listed here to see if other sites have become available.

Work

www.aarp.org
American Association of Retired Persons (AARP): multiple sections, including work

www.adecco.com
Temp staffing

www.ajb.dni.us
America's Job Bank: serious networking

www.careerbuilder.com
Job opportunities and resumé posting

www.careerjournal.com
Executive careers

www.craigslist.com
Jobs

www.dinosaur-exchange.com
Jobs for mature workers

www.directorship.com
Paid corporate board and governance information

www.employmentoffice.net
The World Wide Web employment office

www.execunet.com
Job opportunities

www.fedjobs.com
Search federal jobs

www.freeagent.com
Free agents

www.freelance.com
Freelance work opportunities

www.hotjobs.com
Job search

www.indeed.com
Job search

www.jobhuntersbible.com
Richard Bolles's *What Color Is Your Parachute?* site

www.jobs4point0.com
Job opportunities

www.jobweb.com
Post a resumé and find a job

www.kellyservices.com
Temp staffing

www.manpower.com
Temp staffing

www.monster.com
Monster board

www.parttimejobs.com
Source for hourly employment

www.retiredbrains.com
Helping older workers find jobs

www.retiredjobs.com
Job opportunities

www.seniorjobbank.com
Job opportunities

www.seniors4hire.com
Career center 50+

www.spherion.com
Temp staffing

www.uschamber.org
The Chamber of Commerce directory

www.vocationvacations.com
Try a dream vocation on vacation

www.wetfeet.com
Make smarter career decisions

www.yourencore.com
Job opportunities

www.zerochaos.com
Contract labor solutions

Entrepreneurs

www.entrepreneur.com
Resources for entrepreneurs

www.sba.org
Tips on starting, expanding, and financing your business

www.score.org
Service Corps of Retired Executives, counselors to America's small businesses

Salary Information

www.bls.gov
U.S. Department of Labor, Bureau of Labor Statistics

www.homefair.com
Cost of living calculator and moving information

www.salary.com
Salary information

Volunteer/Not-for-Profit

www.americorps.org
Domestic Peace Corps, VISTA

www.ashoka.org
Information for social entrepreneurs

www.boardnetUSA.org
Connects nonprofit boards and new leaders

www.civicventures.org
A source for learning about individual and social renewal

www.escus.org
Executive Service Corps

www.essential.org
Essential Information encouraging activism

www.experiencecorps.org
Experience Corps engages the time, talent, and experience of older Americans in community service

www.ghostranch.org
Let our world change your world

www.globalvolunteers.org
International volunteers combine service and vacation

www.habitat.org
Habitat for Humanity International

www.idealist.org
Global paid and volunteer jobs

www.IESC.org
International Executive Service Corps

www.networkforgood.org
Helps people connect with a cause

www.peacecorps.org
Peace Corps

www.pointsoflight.org
Points of Light Foundation: local volunteer centers

www.rotary.org
A global network of community volunteers

www.seniorcorps.org
Corporation for National Service: Senior Corps

www.sherrylansingfoundation.org
Committed to making the world a better place

www.volunteermatch.org
A service that matches you to volunteer opportunities

Education and Resources

usm.maine.edu/olli/national
Osher Lifelong Learning Institutes

www.elderhostel.org
Elderhostel

www.unca.edu/ncccr
North Carolina Center for Creative Retirement, Asheville, North Carolina

www.nsu.newschool.edu/irp
The New School's Institute for Retired Professionals

www.SeniorNet.org
Computer technology and Internet training

www.temple.edu/CIL
Temple University's Center for Intergenerational Learning

Other

www.cRANKy.com
Age relevant search engine

www.eons.com
50+ everything

www.google.com
A great search engine

www.thirdage.com
Community of active older adults

www.yahoo.com
A great search engine

General Interest

www.aoa.dhhs.gov
U.S. Administration on Aging

www.dana.org
Gateway to brain information and resources

www.seniorsite.com
Senior resources

www.wikipedia.com
Free encyclopedia

www.wiredseniors.com
Resource site

Also check local agencies and resources that help people find jobs and state websites for job opportunities, such as www.idaho-works.org.

Appendix C
The Eighty-Five Drivers

#1 Accomplishments—to have accomplishments

#2 Accountability—to be accountable for something

#3 Action—to be "part of the action"

#4 Adventures—to have adventures

#5 Authority—to be an authority figure

#6 Belonging—to have a sense of belonging

#7 Bigger Focus—to focus on something larger than oneself

#8 Boss—to be in charge

#9 Challenges—to be challenged

#10 Competition—to be competitive

#11 Connections—to make connections

#12 Control—to be in control

#13 Creativity—to be creative

#14 Credentials—to get credentials

#15 Current—to be current or "in"

#16 Cutting Edge—to be on the cutting edge

#17 Distraction—to have distractions from everyday life

#18 Ego Boost—to have an ego boost

#19 Energized—to feel energized

#20 Enjoyment—to experience enjoyment

#21 Escape—to escape from reality

#22 Excitement—to have excitement

#23 Experiment—to try things out and explore

#24 Fame—to achieve fame

#25 Financial Independence—to achieve financial independence

#26 Friendship—to develop friendships

#27 Fulfillment—to be fulfilled

#28 Fun—to have fun

#29 Game—to view business as a game

#30 Global—to have global opportunities

#31 Goals—to have and to share goals

#32 Identity—to have an identity or sense of self

#33 Importance—to be important

#34 Influence—to be able to have a position of influence

#35 Inspiration—to be inspired by or to inspire others

#36 Intellectual Stimulation—to be with intellectually stimulating people

#37 Joy—to gain a sense of joy

#38 Leadership—to be a leader

#39 Lifelong Learning—to be constantly learning

#40 Lifestyle—to enhance or support my lifestyle

#41 Making a Difference—to help make the world better

#42 Mentoring—to mentor others

#43 Money—to make money as a means to measure success

#44 Needed—to feel needed

#45 Newness/Novelty—to have new experiences

#46 Obligations—to fulfill obligations

#47 Passion—to pursue a passion

#48 People—to have exposure to people

#49 Perks—to get perks and travel and entertainment

#50 Personal Reward—to feel personally rewarded

#51 Player—to be a player

#52 Power—to wield power

#53 Praise—to get praise, credit, and glory

#54 Prestige—to obtain prestige

#55 Problem-Solving—to be a problem-solver

#56 Professional Gratification—to get professional kudos

#57 Promotions—to get promotions and performance recognition

#58 Reason for Being—to have a reason to get up in the morning

#59 Recognition—to be recognized

#60 Relationships—to develop relationships

#61 Respect—to earn family respect

#62 Respect—to get respect from others

#63 Responsibility—to have responsibility

#64 Ritual—to live according to a ritual

#65 Satisfaction—to get satisfaction

#66 Self-Esteem—to enhance self-esteem

#67 Sense of Self—to have sense of self enhanced

#68 Service—to be of service to others

#69 Skills and Talent—to develop skills and talent

#70 Social Acceptance—to be socially accepted

#71 Social—to be connected to others

#72 Spiritual Growth—to be part of something larger

#73 Stage—to have a stage upon which to perform

#74 Structure—to have structure

#75 Success—to be considered successful according to some measure of success

#76 Support—to have a support system

#77 Take Risks—to take risks

#78 Team Spirit—to have team spirit

#79 Time—to fill time

#80 Title—to have a title

#81 Travel—to travel and be worldly

#82 Upward Mobility—to have upward mobility through promotions

#83 Value—to give value or to be valued

#84 Visibility—to have visibility

#85 Worth—to get self-worth

Notes

Chapter 1

[1] Gardyn, Rebecca. "Retirement Redefined," *American Demographics*. November 2000, p. 52.

[2] Rimer, Sara. "Enjoying the Ex-Presidency? Never Been Better," *New York Times*. February 16, 2000, p. H-1.

[3] "Meeting of the Minds: Peter Drucker and Peter Senge Discuss the Future." *Across the Board*, the magazine of The Conference Board, November/December 2000, p. 17.

[4] Gilbert, Susan. "New Portrait of Retiring Is Emerging." *New York Times*. May 29, 2001, p. F7. (The study of 534 married couples was published in "Couples' Work/Retirement Transitions, Gender, and Marital Quality" by Phyllis Moen, Jungmeen E. Kim, and Heather Hofmeister, *Social Psychology Quarterly*, March 2001.)

[5] Handy, Charles. *The Age of Unreason*. Harvard Business School Press, 1989, p. 208.

Chapter 2

[1] Hubler, Eric. "The New Faces of Retirement." *Sunday New York Times*. January 3, 1999.

[2] Weintraub, Pamela. "Finding the Fountain of Youth." August 8, 2001, www.mygeneration.org/departments/2001/health/0705_a.html.

[3] Sadler, William A. *The Third Age: Six Principles for Growth and Renewal After Forty*. Perseus Publishing, 2000, p. 17.

[4] Rosen, Jan M. "The Other Retirement Choice." *New York Times*. August 1, 1999, pp. 3–10.

[5] Hilsenrath, Jon E. "Retirees Becoming Wealthier, Healthier." *Wall Street Journal.* May 12, 2001, p. A-2.

[6] Rosen, Jan M. "The Other Retirement Choice." *New York Times.* August 1, 1999, pp. 3–10.

[7] Carter, Jimmy, and Rosalynn Carter. *Everything to Gain: Making the Most of the Rest of Your Life.* Random House, 1987, p. 62.

[8] Handy, Charles. *The Age of Unreason.* Harvard Business School Press, 1989, pp. 184–185.

[9] Handy, Charles. *The Age of Unreason.* Harvard Business School Press, 1989, pp. 185–186.

[10] Handy, Charles. *The Age of Unreason.* Harvard Business School Press, 1989, p. 173.

[11] www.census.gov/compendia/statab/labor_force_ employment_earnings/, Table 574 "Civilian Labor Force and Participation Rates With Projections: 1980 to 2014"

[12] Rosen, Jan M. "The Other Retirement Choice." *New York Times.* August 1, 1999, pp. 3–10.

[13] Rimer, Sara. "Enjoying the Ex-Presidency? Never Been Better," *New York Times.* February 16, 2000, p. H-1.

[14] Gardyn, Rebecca. "Retirement Redefined," *American Demographics.* November 2000, p. 52. (Having a "new job" refers to being employed for 12 months or fewer.)

[15] Gardyn, Rebecca. "Retirement Redefined," *American Demographics.* November 2000, p. 52.

[16] Shellenbarger, Sue. "Work and Family." *Wall Street Journal.* May 23, 2001, p. B-1.

Chapter 3

[1] Gardyn, Rebecca. "Retirement Redefined," *American Demographics.* November 2000, p. 52.

Chapter 4

[1] Kushner, Harold. *Living a Life That Matters.* Alfred A. Knopf, 2001, p. 6.

[2] www.wfu.edu/wfunews/2001/052101g-b.htm.

Chapter 5

[1] Canavor, Natalie, and Joyce Litwin Zimmerman. "Redefining Retirement." *Newsday.* August 21, 2001, p. B10.

Chapter 6

[1] Rosen, Jan M. "The Other Retirement Choice." *New York Times.* August 1, 1999, pp. 3–10.

[2] "The New Workforce: Knowledge Workers Are the New Capitalists." *The Economist.* November 3, 2001, p. 11.

Chapter 7

[1] Canavor, Natalie, and Joyce Litwin Zimmerman. "Redefining Retirement." *Newsday.* August 21, 2001, p. B10.

[2] "Skadden Arps Series for Women," Skadden, Arps, Slate, Maegher, and Flom LLP. Four Times Square, New York, New York, November 1, 2001. The personal interview occurred in 2002.

[3] Canavor, Natalie, and Joyce Litwin Zimmerman. "Redefining Retirement." *Newsday.* August 21, 2001, p. B10.

[4] Gardyn, Rebecca. "Retirement Redefined," *American Demographics.* November 2000, p. 52.

[5] Carter, Jimmy. *The Virtues of Aging.* Ballantine Publishing Group, 1998, p. 70.

[6] Rosenblatt, Roger. *Rules for Aging: Resist Normal Impulses, Live Longer, Attain Perfection.* Harcourt, Inc., 2000.

Chapter 8

[1] Online interview with Richard Bolles and Steve Willey, financial and career editor, www.myprimetime.com, January 11, 2001.

[2] Schoofs, Mark. "Spotting AIDS in Africa Shaped Doctor's Destiny." *Wall Street Journal.* May 30, 2001, p. B1.

Chapter 9

[1] Hirschman, Carolyn. "Exit Strategies." *HR Magazine.* December, 2001, p. 52. For a fuller discussion of working while receiving a pension, see Chapter 12.

[2] Harkness, Helen. *Don't Stop the Career Clock: Rejecting the Myths of Aging for a New Way to Work in the 21st Century.* Palo Alto, CA: Davies-Black, 1999, p. 2.

Chapter 10

[1] Fried, Joseph P. "He's Too Busy to Call It Retirement." *New York Times.* July 15, 2001, p. 25.

Chapter 12

[1] Brock, Fred. "Slow to Learn the Lessons of Ageism." *New York Times.* December 2, 2001, section 3, p. 9.

[2] Harkness, Helen. "Creating Lifespan Balance: Redefining Career Success and Reinventing Retirement." International Career Development Conference 2000, pp. 39–43.

[3] Olson, Elizabeth. "Small Business: In Life's Second Act, Some Take on a New Role: Entrepreneur." *New York Times.* September 28, 2006, Section C, p. 6.

Chapter 13

[1] Hardy, Michael. "Partnership to Feds: Hire Retired Private-Sector Workers." FCW.com. January 10, 2007.

[2] Kanchier, Carole. "Career Pros: Mature Worker Myths and Realities." *California Job Journal.* January 30, 2005.

[3] Shellenbarger, Sue. "Baby Boomers Already Are Getting Agitated Over Age-Bias Issues." *Wall Street Journal.* May 30, 2001, p. B-1.

[4] Moore, Brian. "The Towers of Babble." *New York Post.* October 9, 2006, pp.38–39.

[5] Strauss, Robert L. "Never Say Never." *Stanford Business Review.* August 2001, p. 18.

[6] Rosenblatt, Roger. *Rules for Aging: Resist Normal Impulses, Live Longer, Attain Perfection.* Harcourt, Inc., 2000, p. 97.

Index

T

U–V

W–X–Y–Z

About the Authors

Jeri Sedlar and **Rick Miners,** a husband and wife team, have 25 years of experience working in the area of personal and professional change. In 1994, they established Sedlar & Miners, an executive search and transition coaching firm, and also wrote their first book, *On Target: Enhance Your Life and Ensure Your Success.* Since then, they have traveled the country delivering keynote addresses and seminars that motivate organizations and individuals to examine themselves as they prepare for the future.

Now, Rick and Jeri have coined the phrase *REWIRE*™ and pioneered the concept of *REWIREMENT*®—or as they call it, the "new way to do retirement." Jeri and Rick work with organizations and individuals who need inspiration and solutions on how to leverage the talents of a never before seen group of retirees! Their mission is to help people make the most of the "longevity bonus," the additional 20 to 25 years after the age of 65, and to help break the "silver ceilings" that exist in organizations.

Jeri is senior adviser to The Conference Board on the Mature Workforce and is a judge for AARP's annual award program: the Best Employers for Workers over 50. Rick is the cofounder of FlexCorpSystems, a business process outsourcing company specializing in third-party employment, cited by *INC. Magazine* as one of the fastest-growing privately held companies in America. When sold in 2006, the firm employed more than 900 individuals, 30 percent of whom were retirees coming back into the workforce.

Jeri and Rick are frequently quoted in the *The Wall Street Journal, The New York Times,* and many other business publications. They have appeared on *The Today Show, NBC Nightly News,* CNN, and PBS, and other media. The authors write for EONS.com, a website targeted to the 50+ population, and are contributing writers to Horsesmouth, a financial newsletter.

For more information on Jeri and Rick's presentations and services, as well as motivational tips, *REWIREMENT*® guidance, and rolling research, please visit www.dontretirerewire.com. Read about their inspiring and customized programs for individuals, organizations, corporations, and couples. Jeri and Rick want to hear from you, so please contact them at authors@dontretirerewire.com.